East of Varley Head

For my dear wife Maria,
without whose unflagging support and encouragement
this book would not have happened.
With love.

James Platt

EAST OF VARLEY HEAD

Stories from Port Isaac, North Cornwall, 1944–1950

First published in Great Britain in 2003 by
Creighton Books
(email: jim.platt@planet.nl)

© 2003 James Platt

ISBN 90 807808 1 2

The moral right of James Platt to be identified as
the author of this work has been asserted by him
in accordance with the Copyright, Designs and
Patents Act 1988

British Library Cataloguing in Publication Data
A catalogue record for this book is available from
the British Library

Designed in the UK by
Special Edition Pre-Press Services

Printed and bound in Great Britain by
Lightning Source UK Ltd

Front cover photograph:
Sunset behind Varley Head, North Cornwall
Back cover photograph:
The author in 1946

Contents

List of Illustrations

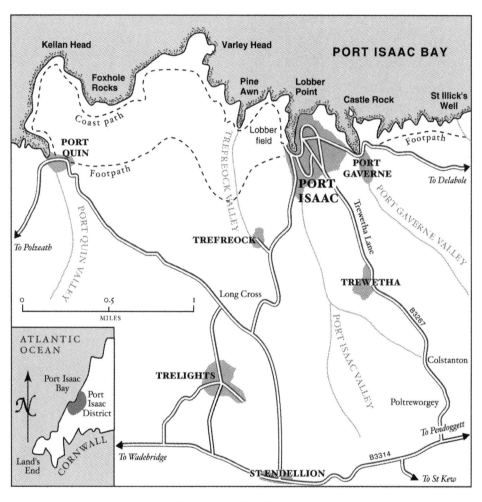

Sketch map of Port Isaac district

vii

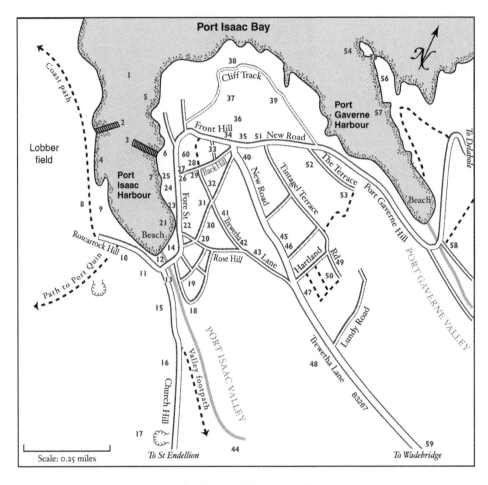

Sketch map of Port Isaac village

Key to numbered locations

1. The awn and Kenewal rock
2. Western breakwater
3. Eastern breakwater
4. Lobber cliff
5. Pink pool
6. Hillson's dump
7. Long pool
8. Khandalla
9. The allotments
10. Residence of Teddy and Mary Hosking
11. Roscarrock Methodist Chapel
12. Pawlyn's cellars
13. The Lake and Middle Street
14. The Town Platt
15. Residence of Mr Edgar Bate
16. Residence of Miss Jessie Pidler
17. Disused quarry (Church Hill)
18. Wesleyan Methodist Chapel
19. Dolphin Street
20. Residence of Mr Westlake Brown and Miss Alice Brown
21. The Pentice
22. Mr Altair Bunt's fruiterer's shop
23. Mr William John Honey's barber's shop
24. Little Hill and Chapman's grocer's shop
25. Port Isaac County Primary School
26. The Liberal Club
27. The Old Drug Store
28. St Peter's church
29. Residence of Doctor Sproull
30. Margaret's Lane
31. Mr Harold Spry's coal yard and garage
32. Residence of Miss Furze
33. Bellevue Terrace
34. The Church Rooms
35. Garage of Mr Charlie Lobb
36. The Rivoli cinema
37. The new coastguard station
38. Wartime (and post-war) coast watcher's hut
39. The vicarage
40. J. N. Hicks & Son butcher's shop
41. The Temperance Hall
42. "First and Last"
43. The fish jouder's cellars
44. Top Shed
45. The National bus garage
46. The Co-op
47. The old council houses
48. The prefabs
49. Residence of Mr Jack Spry
50. Residence of Mr Arthur Dinner and Mrs Gladys Dinner
51. The Prout brothers' "Trelawney" garage
52. The Lawns Hotel
53. St Andrew's Hotel
54. Castle Rock
55. The Gut
56. The Port Gaverne Main
57. Teague's ("Tagg's") pit
58. Port Gaverne Hotel
59. Trewetha Farm
60. Canadian Terrace

The awn and Port Isaac inner harbour

Foreword

Any traveller in North Cornwall who chose to turn his back on the blighted hope of the village of Port Quin, so as to proceed east along the coastal footpath following the rim of the wet black slate cliffs of Port Isaac Bay, would, a mile or so after passing by the prominence of Varley Head, come upon the village of Port Isaac.

The pronunciation of "Varley" rhymed with "fairly". Perhaps the word "Varley" was a corruption of "fair lee", for a fair lee truly was what Varley Head offered the needy.

Varley Head held a beautiful little beach of golden sand on its eastern and sheltered side. More than a few fishermen had had cause to give thanks to an eternal father strong to save for the opportunity to drop an anchor for a while over the comparative calm of Varley Sands. There they could gird up the resources of their little boats for the rough and rugged run back across the Bay to Port Isaac harbour.

The traveller would observe, depending on any well held personal prejudices, that the village of Port Isaac, with a population of near enough one thousand, was either tidily clustered or untidily sprawled around a harbour sharp enough and deep enough to have been formed from the bite of an almighty axe swung at the cliffs by a sea god with nothing better to do.

Where it opened into the Atlantic Ocean, the outer part of Port Isaac harbour, better known as the awn, was guarded on one side by the salient of Lobber Point and on the opposite side by the Kenewal rock. Lobber Point was always a visible and commanding presence, provided that it was not obscured by fog. The Kenewal rock had to count on a tide at very low ebb for its kelp-stubbled jaw to break surface.

The inner harbour was almost spanned by a pair of battered concrete breakwaters. Inside the breakwaters the little fleet of fishing boats was moored in comparative shelter. The breakwaters might not have been as effective as they ought to have been in doing what they should have done, but they didn't lack character. In these qualities they had much in common with Port Isaac people.

———

The tales in this book are all concerned with the village of Port Isaac and its people in the years just before the end of the war and for a little while after it. The breakwaters were at that time maybe no more than twenty years old. The war was the one that took place between 1939 and 1945, and don't you forget it! None of the Port Isaac boys who grew up in the slanting shadow of the post-war years were allowed ever to forget it, and that was a fact they lived with every day.

The recollections on which the tales are based are mine own. They are drawn from the unforgettable experiences of being there at the time. Although I can't pretend that I was not subjective in what I felt when it happened to me, the pages of this book present, with never less than fairness and good humour, exactly what it was that I saw, heard, touched and tasted when I was there.

The tales seek to preserve and celebrate the wonderful memory of many specific and a whole host of related aspects of both Port Isaac life as she was lived and the Port Isaac people, not least the Port Isaac boys, who lived her during the years between 1944 and 1950.

A boy named James moves in and out of and around about a

number of the tales. He is me, and I am him. Once you are born a Port Isaac boy, you are a Port Isaac boy for life. The boy may well be taken out of Port Isaac, but Port Isaac can never be taken out of the boy.

If I only know one thing, I suppose that's it.

———

I was, I still am, and I always will be a Port Isaac boy. I was born in Port Isaac on the eighth of August 1939. The war hadn't quite started then. By the time the war ended I was, let's see, close to six years old.

The purity of the Port Isaac line that I came from was vested in my grandmother. She was born Eleanor Honey in the Port Isaac of 1884, from which vantage point she could look back over many generations of local inbreeding. After Gran there was some adulteration of the genuine Port Isaac element of my blood, but for what I was, that didn't make me any less a Port Isaac boy.

Gran married James Francis Aloysius Creighton, more commonly known as Jim. He was my grandfather, born in the Toxteth area of Liverpool into a life of crushing poverty, a life riddled rotten by the malign attention of Catholic priests. Granfer ran away from Liverpool when he was not yet thirteen, signed up with a ship, and was a subsequent seafarer for almost half a century. He saw action through three wars and crossed just about every sea and ocean that could be printed on a map.

Granfer's family history was always a mystery to me. He never spoke about it or wanted to speak about it. Roman Catholicism was his great bugbear. Granfer himself was no mystery however. He was a man that it was the privilege of my life to belong to. That I never got to tell him that is a powerful regret that I have to live with.

Gran and Granfer met in Plymouth during the Great War that was supposed to end all wars and didn't. Gran was working in Plymouth as a seamstress; Granfer had docked in port with his ship. After they married, they went to live in Port Isaac, in what was an undoubted stroke of fate in assuring my claim to be a Port Isaac boy with Gran and Granfer as cornerstones of my life.

The address of their cottage in Port Isaac was number seven, Canadian Terrace. An unknown and probably soulless individual sitting somewhere in the district council offices at Wadebridge decided at a later date to change the address of number seven, Canadian Terrace, to the characterless anonymity of number sixty-four, Fore Street, and so it remained until the year 2002, when the cottage was named Creighton Cottage in Gran and Granfer's honour.

Gran and Granfer had only one child, a daughter named Eleanor Bettison, whom they called Betty. Betty, a true Port Isaac girl, was my mother. Granfer's lapsed religious sentiments ensured that Betty was brought up with allegiance to the Church of England, as therefore was I. Gran was steeped in the Anglican tradition of St Peter's church, a building that incidentally frowned down on Canadian Terrace from a level on the hill above.

Betty, and my younger brother Trevor and I lived alongside Gran and Granfer in number six, Canadian Terrace, throughout the war. On every living day we were all in and out of number seven on more occasions than could be counted.

My father, Ernest William, generally known as Bill, was a Cornishman, but as he was born in a part of Cornwall that was not Port Isaac he had to be, I have to admit, classed as something of a foreigner. I was never too sure where Bill came from in the first instance. It was either St Germans in east Cornwall, close to the River Tamar with Plymouth straight across the water, or Rock in north Cornwall on the estuary of the River Camel, facing towards Padstow.

It was at Rock where Bill met Betty. Betty was working at Rock in service to the household of a certain Admiral Rogers. The Admiral may have been a fine man. I don't know because I never met him and never will now. It would, however, give me some satisfaction to be able to tell him what I think of people like him who lived to be served by the less privileged. Bill's family, as I knew them, were a grim and forbidding lot, but I had Betty and Gran and Granfer Creighton so it didn't matter much where Bill came from really.

Bill served in the Royal Navy from entry as a cadet at the age of fourteen until he was invalided out of service as a petty officer at the end of the war. He spent the next several years as a resident of a TB sanatorium at Tehidy near Redruth. His wartime experiences and their legacy ensured that he was a man to whom feelings of tolerance related to virtually any subject never came easily.

———

Granfer never seemed to tire of posing the question to me "Don'tcha know there's a war on?" The query came most frequently when I left any food on my plate, not that that was a regular event, or if I got a rip in any item of my clothes, which was much more likely. What the war had to do with my ass hanging out of my pants, as the expression went, I could never fathom out. Granfer kept asking the same question even when the war was finished. There were just so very many ways to contribute to defeating Hitler.

Bill, when he was at home, had his own favourite catch phrase to direct at my conduct. "I didn't fight no bleddy war so's a little bugger like you could behave like that!" This declaration was in common use by all the other Port Isaac men who had been away to fight, as well as a fair few of those Port Isaac men who hadn't. They laid it down, as thickly and as heavily as they could, that they had made huge sacrifices for the benefit of so many undeserving boys, the little buggers that the boys were, every one of them.

The expected price that the boys had to pay as compensation for the alleged sacrifices was to maintain total obedience in a climate of silence until spoken to by those who had sacrificed so much. When the boys were spoken to, their responses were required to be devoid of opinions. The boys should have shown a spirit of gratitude to the men, but any gratitude they felt tended to be overwhelmed by the crushing burden of imposed guilt that to a greater or lesser extent would never leave them.

———

Port Isaac, for several years following the end of the war, remained the tight and closed community that it had been for the prior half-century, and for all I know probably even further back than that. It was almost a tradition for Port Isaac people to resist any pressure for change right up to the point of bitter inevitability. Those who were born in Port Isaac, like Gran, Betty and me, didn't want change to come along at all, but of course, it did.

The end of food and clothes and petrol rationing, the growing numbers of family cars, and not least the arrival of a television service just in time for the Coronation to be seen in snowy shades of light green, pushed Port Isaac and its people over a watershed and into an uncertain future that left the old way of life expiring for the want of a Good Samaritan who was never going to arrive.

Break, break, break;
On thy cold grey stones, O Sea!
And I would that my tongue could utter,
The thoughts that arise in me.

ALFRED, LORD TENNYSON

The village of Port Isaac

1

Place and Time

THERE IT WAS, scrabbled up against a hard and rocky coast and demanding at least a half hour's walk on the part of anyone who wished to reach the nearest road that was unadorned by a line of grass along its crown.

It was a village named Port Isaac. Port Isaac was secreted away in the mouth of a narrow valley right in behind a little cliff-shrouded harbour. A stream dribbled from the valley and braided itself in thin strings across the harbour beach.

The way that anyone took to enter Port Isaac was pretty much the same as the way they were subsequently compelled to go out again. It made no difference to that reality at all whether the available mode of transport for them was on foot, on the National bus, on one of Prout's buses, on a push bike, or even in a motorcar.

Of course it was not that there was not something of an element of choice involved, although it is unlikely that many residents of the village thought much about that. Of three options offered to reach the main road linking Delabole with Wadebridge, they almost invariably chose to go along the gentle and familiar course of Trewetha Lane and so on up over Poltreworgey Hill.

Port Isaac was a village that seemed designed to be passed by, and as far as travellers were concerned, as often as not the design worked in their favour.

The two alternative routes out of Port Isaac involved either ascending the dauntingly steep Church Hill along the west side of the valley and then winding onwards around a jigsaw puzzle of hedges to St Endellion, or heading out to the east via Port Gaverne and on up Weathered Hill to China Downs.

The problem with these alternatives was that neither was especially practicable for motorcars. An official signpost placed at the top of Church Hill registered impracticability for motors in cast-iron terms.

There were very few among the population of Port Isaac who owned motorcars in any event, so that associated impracticalities were the last things on their minds. It followed that anyone who owned a motorcar had almost by definition to be a foreigner.

"Foreigner" was a term characterised by a total lack of kindness of intent. It was used to effectively blanket each and everyone who had the misfortune to be born outside the boundary of St Endellion parish, within which parish Port Isaac was the only significant centre of population.

From the top of Church Hill the view inland, assuming a vantage point on a hedge to gain extra height, took in the scattered roofs of the hamlets of Trewetha, Pendogget (all of two miles distant), and naturally of St Endellion, the latter being the common destination for nearly all of those who ascended Church Hill.

The square granite tower of the unimaginably ancient parish church at St Endellion stood proud in silhouette a mile or so away from the top of Church Hill, prominent on the height of land. A dark line of wind-wracked Scots pines along a hedge in front of the church failed to hide the church entirely, but fared a lot better with respect to the nearby rector's house.

In the graveyard around St Endellion church, generations of the remains of the Port Isaac born lay in timelessly silenced rows, presided over by memorial chunks of granite or great flags of worked best quality Delabole slate. Such gravestones, said Mr Jim Creighton, were plonked down to provide the final assurance that those resting in the coffins beneath, under a six foot cover of stony clay, would be certain to be held down, never to rise again.

The opposing view out to sea from the top of Church Hill covered a mighty sweep of Port Isaac Bay curving from Varley Head clear around to Tintagel Head. If it was not raining, it might additionally be possible to catch a blink of Lundy Island, floating like a ghost out on the horizon.

On the far side of Lundy Island there was rumoured to be an edge that boats under the control of careless navigators were apt to fall over. Any implied threat of disaster, however, was entirely offset by the fact that no Port Isaac fishing boat was ever going to venture within hailing distance of Tintagel Head, let alone Lundy Island.

The Port Isaac born were not worried about falling over any edge anywhere, out at sea or not. They were blessed not only with essentially no motivation at all to set foot outside the parish boundary, but also with very little desire to leave the village precincts behind on any basis at all, even on wheels.

"Foreign travel", anyone who came from Port Isaac was happy to tell any foreigner prepared to listen, "is not for the likes of we".

To come from Port Isaac it was essential to have been born in Port Isaac. Those who were thereby intentionally or accidentally honoured were rarely loath to demonstrate a remarkable lack of reluctance to so inform anyone who wasn't. A special form of gloating was reserved for passing the advice on to foreigners who spoke in accents that had little of Cornwall about them.

If anyone happy to be numbered among the Port Isaac born held any regard for foreigners, it was normally kept buried good and deep. It was the bounden duty of the former to be ready in an instant to do the latter down. In the absence of any foreigners to do down, the Port Isaac born were quite adept at undermining themselves, by which means they kept their skills adequately honed.

There were many occasions when foreigners in Port Isaac were scarcer than no bananas. This state of affairs was most common during the autumn and winter of the year, when it was claimed that anyone firing a gun down Fore Street would be sure of hitting not a single foreigner (although some thought it would be worth trying anyway just in case).

Virtually all of the genuinely Port Isaac born were blood related, although at various degrees of removal. The web of intermarriage snaring most Port Isaac families was tangled beyond any capability of its ever being unravelled. Interbreeding and inbreeding struggled against one another for supremacy. Family trees were impenetrable thickets, badly in need of judicious coppicing.

If God had not seen fit to provide the majority of the Port Isaac born with motorcars for their personal use, he had at least had the ingenuity to give each of them a pair of feet. By this means they were well able to follow the crashing coastline all along the line of Port Isaac Bay.

The direction they went in, whether up or down the coast from Port Isaac, was immaterial. One way was much the same as the other. Over to the west there were only the ravaged remains of Port Quin village to be reached, and up the coast to the east the derelict quarry at Donkey's Hole was about the best that could be offered in the way of ultimate destination.

For that matter there was really nothing much to see on the way along the coast at all, apart that is from dark and mighty slate cliffs, an ocean creaming over tumbled rocks, gulls wheeling and screaming, sea pinks studding springy green cushions, and grass combed into flat order by barbarous gales.

For those who preferred walking out of Port Isaac surrounded by a less boisterous climate than the coastline offered them, the valley fingering back from the harbour supplied, season permitting, flat marshy bottoms thick with yellow irises, cool woods carpeted with bluebells, more running rabbits than could be counted, warm rounded slopes crusted with golden gorse, and tangled brambles drooping under the weight of glossy blackberries.

The little stream in the heart of the Port Isaac valley ran over slippery brown pebbles, gently flicking fronds of watercress with muted currents in its deeper pools. The stream water was good to drink all along its tinkling length – until it reached Port Isaac that is, and was constrained in a channel along and under Middle Street. In those stone-walled confines the tamed stream, which had by then assumed a function as the repository for any and all varieties of waste from surrounding households, was known as "the Lake".

———

Port Isaac was considered by its residents to be first and foremost a fishing village. Local farmers might well dispute that under-standing, but since there was little or nothing that local farmers were not prepared to dispute at the drop of a stained flat cap, their opposition could be easily dismissed by all who knew better.

The harbour was the focal point around which life revolved. The cottages of the village crowded in a slaty jumble, made almost agreeable by the caress of time, around the sharp edges of the inner harbour and its guardian breakwaters. Outside the breakwaters, the deep awn, the outer harbour, opened its arms to the ocean.

The breakwaters were adorned below the high-tide mark by prolific hosts of limpets, and were otherwise decorated above the high tide mark by a long-standing application of gull shit. The soaring and shadowed grandeur of Lobber cliff on the west side of the harbour loomed over the western breakwater like a protecting spirit.

A score of little wooden fishing boats tugged at tar-stiffened mooring ropes in the harbour when the tide was in, or alter-natively lay on their sides on the coarse wet sand when the tide was out.

When they were not out at sea, which seemed to be a fairly frequent occurrence for a lot of them, the fishermen who worked the boats congregated in the vicinity of the Town Platt, up at the head of the harbour. The Town Platt incorporated an area raised up alongside the lifeboat slipway and the adjacent Lake.

———

Across the slipway and the Lake was the long outer wall of Pawlyn's fish cellars. Catches of fish, crabs and lobsters were brought up to Pawlyn's from the fishing boats in great baskets made of woven withies. Inside Pawlyn's cellars the produce was readied for despatch to foreign parts, not excluding Padstow.

The fishermen gathered together seemed to vie with one another as to whose close-proximity odour was the most pungent, as to who could spit tobacco juice the furthest, especially if targeting a boy, as to who could spin the tallest yarn without being openly accused of being a liar, and as to who could establish himself as a tattered king in a court in which eccentric princes were legion.

Although centred on the Town Platt, this distinctive court was just one element of an extended company of characters spread around Port Isaac village as thickly as a knife-load of treacle drawn across a buttered (or margarined) crust of Sherratt's new bread. Its worthy members could be found loitering in any road, lane, alley and ope that could be imagined, not least at the most unexpected or inconvenient moments.

They stood at, or preferably leaned on, corners, as if to provide reassurance to the passing public that there could be no collapse of the backing masonry as long as their shoulders had any say in the matter. An impressive majority of them feared nothing that did not involve the need to do some work.

For the most part, there was always going to be someone around to scrounge a fag from. Once in a while they could expect to lay their hands on vegetables of some kind that were ready and waiting in gardens and allotments, although not necessarily their own. Gulls eggs came along for the taking in season. Rabbit meat was an accepted food staple, and there were so many rabbits in the fields that any one could go out and catch a couple with ease.

———

Fore Street, Port Isaac, greatly favoured by the indolent, was graced by a chip shop, a newsagent, a greengrocer, a bakery, a public house called The Golden Lion, a post office, a fruiterer (whatever that was), a grocer, a barber, a Liberal Club with a competition-sized billiard table, a public lavatory, and an Old Drug Store bearing a lettered sign in Old English script.

Elsewhere in Port Isaac village were to be found the premises of a cobbler, a shoe shop, a Co-op specialising in groceries and drapery, a dairy, a couple of butchers, a shoal of fish jouders, a milkman, a coal merchant and a weekly cinema in a converted garage that went under the glorious name of the Rivoli. All the essential elements of self-sufficiency were therefore firmly in place, totally obviating any need for anyone to seek them out in foreign parts.

One butcher's shop was located down in Middle Street. It had a blank wall on the side against the running Lake and another wall pierced by an entry set in a narrow alley connecting across to Church Hill. A second butcher's shop was located in the deep curve of New Road over on the right from the top of Back Hill, run by a father and son for whom time counted for nothing. This was a sentiment not shared by all of their customers.

———

New Road made a tight loop at the top of Back Hill, and then headed out towards Port Gaverne Hill, first passing a tangle of active garages on the left (chief among which was the Prout brothers' Trelawney garage) before, ultimately, leading by the great array of hotels and boarding houses along the Terrace on the right.

The Terrace made a bleak prospect in the winter. It was in winter, when last summer's visitors were but a fading memory, that the booking deposits of next summer's batch of visitors were awaited by hotel proprietors with a grasping eagerness when each day's delivery of post was due.

Port Isaac's spiritual needs were satisfied by St Peter's church, a barn–like building standing adjacent to an abandoned and closed–in mine shaft about half way up Back Hill, and by two Methodist chapels right down at the bottom of the village. The two chapels, named Roscarrock and Wesley, were as implacable in the disdain their respective congregations held for each other as they were in their jointly disunited front opposing the church of St Peter.

The Port Isaac boys wove their daily way like errant threads through the bright tapestry of characters, through tight and spidery streets, close valleys, open fields, wild cliffs, rocky coves, welcoming apple orchards, rookeries, quarries, fish cellars, gardens and allotments.

The four central and revered pillars of wisdom that supported, and tried with mixed fortunes to hold such boys in line, were the County Primary School Headmaster, Mr C. Victor ("Boss") Richards; the vicar of St Peter's, the Rev. W. Atterbury Thomas; the family doctor, Dr Sproull; and the policeman, Mr Pearce, who lived up at Trewetha.

With practised regularity, the boys dodged attempts not only by specific members of the four pillars, but also by irate farmers, intolerant fishermen and unappreciative elders and betters, to clip their ears or tan their asses either on the grounds of misdeeds real or alleged, or more simply just to encourage them in the lessons of life.

Few patterns of behaviour on the part of any of the boys failed in not drawing a comment from one or other of these elders to the effect that the latter had not fought a war, irrespective of the truth of the assertion, to allow little buggers to behave in that way.

The boys' year clicked by in a well-loved and well-established routine. Each season brought along specific activities that were essential to the proper flow of time. The boys prospected for bird's eggs, hunted for sea-tossed wreck, picked baskets of blackberries, posies of primroses and armfuls of bluebells, lounged in the sun, chased rabbits, swam in the harbour, dug in the sand, fished off the rocks, built camps and fought each other amicably at the drop of a balaclava helmet.

Buds swelled, leaves spread, greened, yellowed and fell. Snow lay in stark lines on blackened branches. Icicles dripped from the cliffs. Fog obscured reason. Apples were scrumped; playground games broke up in satisfying fights. Trees and cliffs were climbed. The first gull's egg of the season was eaten. Rabbits and blackberries went into pies, although not necessarily into the same pie.

There was Easter, the long summer holiday, Harvest Thanksgiving, Guy Fawkes Day, Remembrance Sunday, and the long and wonderful anticipation and final blessing of Christmas, carol singing and the Sunday school party.

There were the *Beano* and the *Dandy*, *Adventure* and the *Wizard* to read. There were Larry the Lamb and Norman and Henry Bones to listen to on the wireless.

There were insoluble family feuds, battles between sharp-tongued neighbours, the hiding away from itinerant gypsies and the rent man, the milk delivered in a bucket and dipped up out of the bucket into a basin. There were cream, pasties and pea soup.

———

Traditionally, the boys' elders and betters believed that they, the elders and betters, merited an attitude of respectful servility by the boys. Those among the elders and betters who, in the boys opinion, deserved the boys' respect (there were not an awful lot of them) sometimes got it.

For the most part the boys' elders were the Port Isaac born, whereas their betters tended to be set apart by their elders as foreigners. In principle the Port Isaac born element, who were poor, were required to be deferential to the foreign breed, who were not.

———

In all the tight warp and weft of the tapestry of Port Isaac there was little fraying, although such fraying as there was was significant. Life was a colour wash of place, time, people, circumstances and rippling consequences. It progressed within a contained world lined with incidents, seasoned with momentary dramas and crises, strewn with passages of excitement, sadness, grief, and boredom, and held together by a routine trivial round solely designed, it seemed, to ensure the presence of food on the table.

*View of Varley Head looking across Cartway Cove, the Port Gaverne
Main, Castle Rock and the upper part of Port Isaac*

The pride of Mrs Morman's Class.
FROM LEFT TO RIGHT – *Back row:* Roger Perry, Barwis Bennett, Michael Bate,
Maxie Richards. *Middle row:* Mollie Hooke, Roger Keat, Leonard Honey, James Platt,
Colin Mitchell. *Front row:* Vera Tamsett, Vivienne Donnithorne, Margaret Blake,
Mrs Morman, Anne Thomas

2

Boss

IT MAY DO NO HARM to repeat here that the Headmaster of Port Isaac County Primary School was named Mr C. Victor Richards.

Not a single one of the County Primary School pupils that Mr C. Victor Richards controlled, together with those who he thought he controlled, could have said, even under duress, what the C stood for in the name of Mr C. Victor Richards. They didn't know, and moreover they didn't care.

It was enough that the pupils were induced to be aware, as often as not by way of the pain of personal experience, what Mr C. Victor Richards in his fully named glory stood for. What he stood for was, put simply, no nonsense or the perception of nonsense from any one of them.

Mr C. Victor Richards was the ultimate suit-clad authority for all Port Isaac County Primary School pupils. In the conclave of their own company the pupils named Mr C. Victor Richards "Boss", which was precisely what he was for them beyond any shadow of doubt. By the name of Boss, Mr C. Victor Richards came to be defined and acknowledged throughout the whole Port Isaac community, well abroad of the school.

Mr C. Victor Richards wore the name of Boss as if it were an ornate badge on a cloak of imperial purple confirming his position as a pre-eminent cornerstone of Port Isaac life. Boss expected and deigned to receive respect as his due. From Boss's hands the uncouth were afforded no quarter, and even the couth had to watch their backs when Boss was around.

Boss's wife was named Elsie, but she was better known as Mrs Boss Richards. Mrs Boss was a lady of mercurial character with a bearing of pure brass. She was once overheard to address Boss as "Vic", although in all exchanges with third parties when Boss was not around Mrs Boss never referred to C. Victor as anything other than Boss.

———

Boss and Mrs Boss lived in a house that was an original element of the school buildings. It was presumably tagged on to the aggregation of classrooms for the specific purpose of housing a planned succession of headmasters and their families. The front of Boss's house faced on to the main area of the school playground, and commanded a view, at least from its upper windows, of the deep harbour of Port Isaac, with Lobber cliff and the sweep of Lobber field behind on the far side.

The proximity of the front door of Boss's house to the playground provided an observation platform for Mr and Mrs Boss that did not always create results benefiting the pupils at play, although for his part Boss tended to let any over-exuberant and unscheduled playground activities work themselves to a near standstill before he chose to insert his presence into the melee.

When the all too regular event of a playground fight was in progress, the timing of its suppression depended on whether or not the combatant with the upper hand was favoured by Boss. In cases of particular favour, Boss might not put in any appearance at all.

Mrs Boss's readiness to invade the playground was seldom subdued, however. If her younger son Maxie was a participant, even peripherally, in one or other of the more conflictive scenes that characterised playtimes, Mrs Boss was apt to wade into the fray like Tommy Farr and take no prisoners in rescuing her beloved Maxie.

———

Maxie stood out like a sore thumb in the playground. His face was pink-scrubbed and his fair hair was always combed into the kind of submission that was as close to abject capitulation as any of the other boys could imagine.

Maxie's hands were as grainy skinned as pieces of driftwood. It came from too much washing said the boys, most of whom believed in any case that almost any amount of washing was too much. These boys did their best to avoid grimy contact with Mrs Boss's pristine son, but really that could only be taken so far and no further. Maxie was a target sent to them by heaven, and so the boys felt obliged to do whatever they had to do.

———

Including Boss as its undisputed lord and master, the Port Isaac County Primary School declared a complement of four teachers. Five days per week from nine o'clock in the morning to four o'clock in the afternoon (excluding the so-called infants' class which ran from nine o'clock in the morning to half past three in the afternoon), the four teachers endeavoured to overcome the spirited resistance to learning of the close to four score pupils who were in their combined charge.

It was acknowledged not only by the pupils, but also more universally by their elders and betters, that Boss and his teachers had been placed at the school by virtue of divine authority. The twin commandments handed down to the teachers, on what must have been tablets of stone, instructed them to teach and to dispense discipline to the pupils, not necessarily in that order of priority.

Whatever occurred to pupils or was otherwise visited upon them at school within school hours was, according to their elders and betters, a matter for the teachers and the pupils to sort out between themselves.

No matter how summary was the discipline meted out to a pupil inside the school gates, tales were seldom told outside. There was no question in the minds of the teachers, the elders and betters, and not improbably the pupils as well, but that every last scrap of discipline handed down by the former to the latter was richly deserved.

Boss cut a rather unlikely figure as a disciplinarian. He was of no more than average height and build. Compared to some of the heftier big boys who sat (and sat) in his classroom, Boss appeared to be slight of figure. It was the aura of power about him that gave him a stature transcending mere physical size. Big, brash and muscular boys turned into trembling reeds at Boss's approach.

Boss's voice was rounded and commanding, larded with self-confidence, short on sanctimony, and raised only infrequently in anger. Boss was well able to silence a clamorous classroom with the tilt of a single eyebrow, or to freeze a turbulent playground into submission with the twitch of a finger.

Boss had the jut of an ambitious army captain all too eager for promotion. His gleaming, slicked-back hair was no stranger to liberal applications of Brylcreem. He sported a tight little moustache bristling over sharp teeth that he bared alarmingly when the occasion called for subordinates to be dressed down.

Customarily, Boss carried a yard-long whippy bamboo cane in his right hand, holding the device as if it was a natural extension of his arm. He habitually flicked the cane gently and rhythmically against his suited leg while his scouring eyes searched around for the kind of mischief-makers that he could test the cane on.

For all that, Boss carried the cane more as a promise than as an immediate threat. The cane was a deterrent rather than a weapon, its function being largely ceremonial. Tibby Thomas claimed that Mo Tamsett once received six of the best with the cane from Boss, but only Boss and Mo knew for sure if this really happened, and since neither of them ever said anything there was only Tibby's word to go on.

Boss wielded his cane as a goad to maintain a crisp integrity in the class-specific assembly lines that formed up in the playground by decree at the end of each playtime. Following Boss's inspection, the lines marched to their classrooms with, well almost, military precision.

Any trailing hands or prominent backsides that detracted from the symmetry of the assembly lines were reasonably sure to be stung into instant retraction by the wasp-like tip of Boss's cane.

—

The pupils were absolutely clear in their understanding that for them to attend school, to be taught while they were at school, and to be clipped around the ear by a teacher or flicked by Boss's cane from time to time was their bounden duty. Truancy was something that existed only in stories.

Fathers missed no opportunity to inform their offspring that the assurance of this bounden duty was yet another reason (of many, so many more) why they, the fathers, had recently fought a war.

An absence of a pupil from school therefore implied that if the said pupil was not dead, he or she was either at least too sick to walk, or otherwise unable to leave home owing to his or her only pair of boots being temporarily in the hands of Mr Harry Morman. Harry was the Port Isaac cobbler, and regarded time as something made by God in an unlimited supply.

The pupils wound their weekday routes to the school from all over the length and breadth of Port Isaac village and the surrounding district, homing in like pigeons from surrounding farms and hamlets. Some came in from regions as far flung as Trewetha and Trelights.

No extremes of weather could halt any pupil's routine of passage. Rain, hail, gales or snow were all trudged through in a spirit of valiant resignation. As far as the pupils saw it, they were doing no more than what was expected of them.

Boss received the pupils in the formal demesne of the assembly lines with a pride that he didn't always elect to show. He cherished each pupil's company from behind a self-constructed wall of well-groomed reserve. He entered into their hearts, even though they didn't know it at the time. They made progress in being educated in spite of themselves.

—

Port Isaac children commenced their schooling in the infants' class at the County Primary School at the age of four or five. Just how old they were when they started depended on the timing of their birthdays with respect to the date on which the autumn term began. Four or five, it didn't matter, as they were condemned to be classified as infants until they moved up to the next class at the age of seven or so.

The infants' class was taught by Miss Smythe. She was comparatively young, although she was not necessarily basking in the first flush of youth. Miss Smythe's approach to teaching was gentle and caring. Her pupils responded to her in kind. Most infants left her class able to read, write, draw a little, have a feel for some of the more interesting stories in the Bible, rattle off the tables up to twelve times, and add, subtract and divide in htu's.

They also became accomplished in swallowing a daily spoonful of cod liver oil in a single gulp without tasting it, and were experts in the surreptitious disposal of the mandatory bottle of too cold milk at morning playtime.

––––

The infants had their own dedicated playground, segregated from the main playground area where Mrs Boss maintained her endless vigil for Maxie's well being and hygiene, by a high wall built of blocks of slate. Whoever designed the wall evidently acted on the principle that it would hold the big boys out and keep the little boys in, omitting in his zeal to appreciate that to Port Isaac boys any wall, anywhere, was an open challenge to be tackled and overcome.

The games in the main playground were, not without some justification, considered to favour the kind of rough element to which delicate infants ought not to be exposed, notwithstanding that there were among the infants those who were quite capable of holding their own outside school in much rougher society and conditions than the main playground could ever throw at them.

––––

The second class of Port Isaac County Primary School, to which the infants graduated at the age of seven, and in which they remained until achieving the age of nine brought them some blessed relief, was taught by Mrs Morman. She was, incidentally, the wife of Harry, the cobbler.

However sceptical Mrs Morman might have been about excuses for non-performance or non-attendance offered up by any of her pupils, she was all too amenable to accept an excuse related to delayed boot repair. She knew only too well that Harry worked at less than lightning speed.

Mrs Morman was a lady of generous proportions. Her figure in silhouette would have been not unfamiliar to admirers of Miss Tessie O'Shea. She commanded her classroom with all the subdued modulation of tone exemplified in any stage performance by Miss Peggy Mount.

On entering Mrs Morman's class the immediate experience for the former infants was akin to them being grabbed while sunbathing and slung off the end of the Eastern breakwater in the harbour at the point of high tide.

Mrs Morman's avoirdupois placed no impediment on her ability to move fast and act with even greater despatch against those who transcended her classroom rules of silence until spoken to (solely by Mrs Morman of course). She demanded submissive decorum at all times. Only the more indomitable spirits were able to rise over and prevail against her daily assault on their individualism.

Brandishing a one-foot long wooden ruler, Mrs Morman endeavoured to fan deeply latent coals of intellect into flame. The flat face of the ruler rose and fell in the manner of a gusting wind on the palms of many forcibly outstretched hands. The thin edge of the ruler rapped against knuckles was an alternative reserved by Mrs Morman for very special transgressors. Her false teeth clacked and spittle flew from the edge of her mouth as she meted out just deserts.

Between them, Mrs Morman and her ruler made a successful enough combination in promoting the further development of reading and arithmetical skills in the pupils of her class. She taught them the rudiments of joined-up writing, and how to use the initially clumsy loops and curls to present dictated words and elementary compositions on the ink-spattered pages of ragged exercise books. She was good at religious instruction as well, and must have absorbed that talent from Harry, who sometimes taught Sunday school at the Wesley chapel.

Harry's legendary deafness made him a highly popular Sunday school teacher with chapel boys. Whereas the boys who went to St Peter's church were required to learn and recite their weekly texts to a Sunday school teacher whose sense of hearing could detect a rat in an organ pipe from the far end of the nave, in order to keep Harry happy the boys who attended chapel Sunday school had merely to ensure that their lips moved when he called upon them.

Mrs Morman was inevitably thought of as "Old Ma Murphy, the strong arm school ma'rm", a character whose exploits regularly graced the pages of the *Dandy* comic. Her pupils fervently believed that in a contest Mrs Morman could beat Old Ma Murphy hollow on any day of the week. In fact, when they came to think of it, Mrs Morman would have made a good match for Old Ma Murphy's *Dandy* companion, "Desperate Dan".

—

Following their discharge from the servitude of Mrs Morman's class at the age of nine, the Port Isaac County Primary School pupils fell into the congenial hands of Mr Perry for the next two years. These were critical years since at the end of them the dreaded eleven-plus examination was scheduled.

The results of the eleven-plus examination provided a manifest example of how many were called but few were chosen. The results determined the identity of the few pupils who would continue their schooling thereafter at Sir James Smith's Grammar

School, ten miles away in Camelford, and, by default, of the greater balance who would go on to join Boss's class.

———

Mr Perry was a young man with a style that, for Port Isaac, came dangerously close to being flamboyant. He was totally without rancour and had a flair for fun that from time to time almost made him one of the boys. The boys loved him. Boss maybe didn't. Mr Perry moved his pupils' minds several steps further along the dark tunnel of learning towards a barely perceived light at its end, introducing them to arts and crafts, to geography, to history, to decimals, fractions and compound interest as well, for those who understood what compound interest was.

Mr Perry was in charge of formally organised team sports, the relationship of which to playground activities was as cheese to chalk, or alternatively as sugar to shit. Every week on a given afternoon in the football season, no matter what the wind or weather, he led an array of boys up to the wind-scoured head of Lobber field, where they kicked around a soggy leather ball inflated with a pigs bladder while endeavouring not to place their feet in the fresher pats of cow dung that littered the field of play.

Some boys approached the Lobber field sports sessions with all the enthusiasm of French aristocrats on their way to the guillotine, and returned downhill afterwards as if they were retreating from Dunkirk minus any vestige of Dunkirk spirit.

———

Mr Perry taught the boys how to perform a feat of magic involving a penny and an empty bottle. By virtue of clapping the flat of the penny against a window and simultaneously smashing the bottle on the wall beneath, an irate householder was induced to appear like a genie in no more than an instant. The glory of the trick was that it worked every time. It became a most satisfactory alternative to the great game of knocking on doors and running away, which the boys called "knock down dolly", and about which the boys could have taught Mr Perry a few things.

———

21

Those who fell at the fence of the eleven-plus and subsequently entered Boss's class remained under his tutelage until they reached the formal school-leaving age of fifteen. Boss taught art, geometry, classic literature, and the basis of the human condition to red-faced farm boys, to fishermen's sons and to pigtailed, navy blue knickered girls alike.

He instructed them all in the virtues of a life shaped by honesty and humility. It was no easy task. Many of his pupils came from homes that were poor enough to ensure that the pupils maintained a deferential demeanour in the presence of their elders and betters, but poverty and absolute honesty tended to make strange bedfellows.

Boss's creed was to prepare his pupils for what lay in store for them when they left his classroom, aged fifteen, for the last time. That he succeeded in shaping some brilliant cuts from more than a few rough stones, thereby leaving ajar the doors of opportunity for those whose constraint was that they were fated to have been born on the wrong side of the locked gates of privilege, placed a blessed shine on his memory.

*The harbour at low tide, with Lobber cliff on the left and the long slope
down to Lobber Point beyond the breakwaters*

Port Isaac County Primary School in its cliff edge grandeur

3

How the Big Ones Kept the Little Ones In Around

THE MAIN SCHOOL PLAYGROUND was entered through the smaller, upper section of a wooden double gate that was in line with the wall of the old Lifeboat House above Little Hill on Fore Street. The lower, and much bigger section of the gate was normally chained shut, probably to prevent the children swinging on it. Generally the lower section of the gate was only opened to let a vehicle enter the main playground, although such occasions were rare indeed.

The main playground was surfaced with hard tar macadam, a medium that provided a sure guarantee of more skinned knees and elbows than would ever be reliably counted. It completely surrounded the side of the school facing the harbour, wrapping itself right around to and just beyond the school's rear cloakroom entry, where it was brought up short by the high wall that segregated it from the infants' playground. The outer edge of the main playground was coincident with a much lower retaining wall along the edge of the harbour cliff.

Although it was a single continuous entity, the main playground was effectively divided into two sectors by a constriction about ten feet wide between the school building's lower front corner buttress and the cliff wall. By convention, the sector of the playground beyond this bottleneck, which is to say at the back of the school, was known by the children as "in around". The sector of the playground outside the bottleneck, from the front of the school to the Little Hill wall, was then called, not unnaturally, "out around".

The wall along the cliff was three feet high for out around and twice that for in around. Apart from some brave thorny scrub hugging its outer face, that wall was all that lay between the cream of Port Isaac children at playtime and a solid or a watery end below – depending on the state of the tide of course.

Out around was characterised by a perceptible slope from the side of the old Lifeboat House down to the cliff wall. At the crest of the slope, in a corner formed by the edge of the headmaster's house and the top part of the wall of the old Lifeboat House, the girls tended to gather to twirl skipping ropes.

———

Elsewhere in out around, mass action football matches were played out to the very death, with teams numbered in scores surging this way and that and then back again in pursuit of a threadbare tennis ball. Kicking the ball was what mattered, and ultimate allegiance to any particular team was quickly forgotten in the thrill of the chase.

One of the goals was the bottleneck between in around and out around. The other goal was the wall at the bottom end of the playground that separated the playground from Little Hill.

The very same tennis ball that assumed a new life as a playground football – or it could have been one of its near relatives – also did duty as a cricket ball in season. The cricket pitch was set up across the widest part of out around, bowling from the harbour wall end at a wicket chalked on the red brick base of the Old Lifeboat House. The bat was whittled from a suitable piece of driftwood.

In the performance of both cricket and football games the ball inevitably went over the retaining wall, either to lodge in the thorns on the upper part of the cliff below, or finally to end up all the way down on the beach. Lost balls were rare, however, since there were always more than enough volunteers to go over the wall, against the rules but not to worry about that, and retrieve a ball from wherever it lay.

In around was devoted to playtime pursuits other than football and cricket, but anyone who saw in around as a quiet haven in which the threat of contact games could be avoided was soon to be disillusioned.

On the occasions when the big boys of the school did not want to play football, or for that matter couldn't when no ball was available, they gained solace by rounding up the smaller boys, willing or not, for participation in a game with the self-descriptive title of "the big ones keep the little ones in around".

As a precursor to this game, the little ones (the smaller boys) were driven in around and herded together like a submissive flock of sheep by a menacing group of the big ones (the big boys). A second group of the big ones then linked themselves together to form a human wall facing in around across the buttressed bottleneck that separated out around from in around.

With out around blocked off from in around, the big ones who made up the not so good shepherds, by employing the time-honoured device of applying their boots to the backsides and their hands to the ears of the selected little ones, compelled the little ones to charge the restraining wall of big ones that sealed them off from out around. The task of the little ones was to break through the barrier to gain the safe haven of out around. The purpose of the big ones was to stop the little ones by whatever physical means the fracas dictated in the heat of battle.

Once the game was afoot, all players, big ones and little ones alike, entered into the spirit of it, pushing, shoving, punching, scratching and clawing, biting and kicking, anything in the overwhelming desire on the one side to break through, and on the other to hold back the tide.

Although the little ones seldom broke through, there were some days when they did, and those were days of sweet victory that sustained hope in the hearts of the little ones that the big ones were not going to be able to keep them in around forever.

All participants gave of their best, knowing that the signal for the end of playtime would finish the game irrespective of whatever stage of winning or losing it might have reached. The end was never acrimonious.

—

An indoor variation of "the big ones keep the little ones in around" was devised for days when rainfall militated against playground activities. This variation was not inappropriately known as "roughhouse". It owed its inspiration to the glorious bar-room brawls that were such an essential feature of every cowboy film shown up at the Rivoli on Fridays.

The game of roughhouse found its place in the cloakroom located at the back end of in around. It was through this cloakroom that the class lines filed in sequence to their respective classrooms after playground assembly.

To prepare for roughhouse, the big ones invaded and occupied the cloakroom. They closed the inner door leading to the adjacent classroom and blocked the small cloakroom window with jerseys and jackets taken off at random from the cloakroom pegs. A flock of little ones was then gathered and driven into the cloakroom, whereupon the outer door was closed, leaving the cloakroom pretty much in darkness.

Then it was free-for-all action, little ones attacking big ones, big ones attacking big ones, little ones attacking little ones. There were no holds barred, no sides and no quarter given. It was universal pushing, punching out and windmilling arms in the dark. Whoever or whatever was contacted was no more than fair game. Shouts, yells, curses and screams accompanied the action. The bodies of little ones sailed through the air, fetching up against any obstacle that presented itself to the path of flight. Shirts were ripped and noses were bloodied.

At one point the wadded jackets and jerseys blocking out the window either fell down, or more likely were pulled down, and in the dim light of day the mayhem ceased – always, let it be said, in good time for meeting the obligations of assembly.

Although the sudden entry of light into the cloakroom might be considered fortuitous, in all probability it intervened to terminate the roughhouse more as an act of fate.

Roughhouse did not take place too often and so was all the more memorable an event when it did. All involved no doubt pulled their punches more than a little as the game was always characterised by the joy of battle on all sides. When it was over it was over, and those who had been in it were all been glad to have been a part of it.

At the back of in around, in the open part between the rear wall of the school and cloakroom on one side and the lavatories on the other side by the cliff, the game most frequently played was "Cockarusha". The title may have been derived from a corruption of "Cock of Russia", or it may not. No one really knew or, when it came down to it, really cared.

Cockarusha was in every sense a contact game. It had as its objective the passage of players from the school wall across to the lavatories. One by one in sequence the players made the passage, hopping on one foot with their arms folded. To impede the passage, a player selected for his agility and size, also hopping with folded arms, was placed as a guardian in the centre of the field of play.

The guardian's task was to shoulder barge the player intent on hopping across the field of play so as to make the latter fall over or drop his raised foot to the ground. For his part the crossing player was required to barge back or dodge the guardian when attacked, in order to reach safe ground at the far side by the lavatories.

Once his foot fell and touched the ground, a crossing player was "out" and joined the guardian on the field of play, so that the next player in line to hop across was faced with the prospect of having to evade two hopping guardians. And so on.

The first period of cockarusha ended when all players had made one attempt to cross over. The second period required those who had crossed successfully to hop back to the school wall again. This time they were faced by a daunting array of guardians, the original one having been joined by those who failed to make the first crossing.

A game of cockarusha finished when the last foot of the last player trying to cross the field touched the ground. It was a game with a simple and relatively easy beginning, but one that rapidly increased in pace and intensity as the barrier of guardians grew ever greater. In its closing stages cockarusha demonstrated true survival of the fittest.

———

The protruding buttresses on the in around side of the school provided the support for an impromptu playground game named "Squashems". The only ingredient needed for squashems to come alive was for a boy – preference given to his being a member of the little ones – to stand or lean in the corner between a buttress and the school wall.

His real purpose in being there was not material. He might well have been sheltering from the wind whistling through the bottleneck separating in around from out around. He may have been resting. He may have been trying to hide from someone. All that was important was that there he was, with his shoulder up against a buttress and the school wall behind him.

On viewing the standing target lodged in the corner of the buttress and the wall, a second boy, this time almost certainly a member of the big ones, moved in, shouldered up to the former, and endeavoured to shove him sideways through the buttress. Whereupon a third, a fourth and, in the blink of an eye, a whole line of boys joined in the affray, backs to the wall, shoving, pushing and squashing the line laterally like a concertina. Individuals came flying out of the squeezing line of boys, forcibly ejected as if they were peas popping from a pod. They gathered themselves up and hared to the back of the line to join in once more.

Squashems usually ended when enough was enough. The heaving line of boys dispersed as quickly as it had formed. Keen vigilance for spotting the next unfortunate who believed there was refuge in the lee of a buttress made it certain, however, that squashems would be played again.

It was during a session of squashems that the only significant accident known to be directly related to playground games took place, when a certain collarbone proved unequal to the pressure. Following the accident, squashems was banned by Boss Richards. But the best traditions always died hard, and the sight of a potential victim up against a buttress would always provide an opportunity too good for some boys to pass on.

"Rusty Bum" was a much more structured playground game than squashems and relied equally on the backing support of the in around school wall. In rusty bum teams of five or six a side – although the ultimate number was flexible – played against each other. The game demanded strong backs and as much cumulative team weight as possible. Under these criteria, the big ones would always be the masters.

One rusty bum team was passive and one was active. The teams took it in turn to play the passive and active roles. For the passive team, an anchor boy stood with his back hard up against the school wall. The other members of the team formed up in a line facing him, then bent over in sequence from front to back to form a flat-backed single line by virtue of inserting their heads between the legs of the team member ahead of them and gripping his thighs with their arms. The anchor boy gripped the shoulders of the boy at the front of the line for added stability.

The active team then entered the game. One by one they ran at the lined-up backs to vault as far forward along the line as they were able. The passive line was required to withstand the growing weight of bodies lying on its back and hold firm. The winners were the team that held up longest, since the whole line inevitably collapsed sooner or later. If the active team could not collapse the passive line, it simply co-opted more players until the weight was sufficient unto the day.

As a player ran up to vault on to the line of backs he chanted:

Here I come,
Rusty bum,
Two, four, six, eight –
Ten ton!

It was the chant of the advancing players that gave the game of rusty bum its character. The ritual was devoutly practised since the great playground games, be it the big ones keeping the little ones in around, roughhouse, squashems, cockarusha or rusty bum, all thrived on ritual.

There was much comfort to be derived from knowing not only what was going to happen, but also when it would happen, and not least what the sequence of events was likely to bring.

A herring gull on the Pentice wall

Where New Road, Back Hill and Front Hill meet at the Church Rooms

4

Cinema at the Rivoli

IMMEDIATELY TO THE RIGHT of where Bellevue Terrace emerged from its dank and furtive confines into the open light of Back Hill stood the neat cottage of Mr and Mrs Charlie Lobb. A well-trimmed hedge of thick, glossy evergreen bushes, pierced in one place by a small wooden gate, separated Charlie's cottage and its blooming patch of front garden from Back Hill.

Below Charlie's cottage the deep declivity of Back Hill fell steeply downwards, passing by the parish pump at Mine Pit Corner on the left and St Peter's church on the right, and making an eventually arresting junction with Fore Street between the Old Drug Store and the Liberal Club.

It was rumoured that the cutting in which Back Hill lay was excavated long ago by a squad of convicts. Normally resident in the rigorous Dartmoor Prison, the convicts were transported down to Port Isaac to perform the task. The very same arrow-decorated gentlemen were, the rumour mongers declared, those who constructed the slate jetty and associated access tracks out at Port Gaverne, just around the cliffs to the east of Port Isaac. Some others said nothing since they didn't know.

The evergreen bushes that Charlie – unless it was Charlie's father-in-law Mr Roseveare who did it – had managed to tame into such a presentable hedge fronting Charlie's cottage were considerably less controlled in their rampant growth down along the fringe of Back Hill. They lined the descent in a creeper-tangled riot of wild abandon all the way down to the entry path to St Peter's church.

The prospect of Back Hill above Charlie's cottage was devoid of greenery, apart that is from a partially grassed bank towards the top, over on the right hand side. On the left, Back Hill was occupied all the way to its top, where it participated in a three-way junction with Front Hill and New Road, by a gaunt terrace of tall, stony houses that were for the most part quite without character.

———

Charlie, a gruff but kindly man with a common touch, was the proprietor and manager of an untidy accumulation of garages and lockups that sprawled around and behind the outer curve of the three-way junction, from which nexus New Road took off towards Port Gaverne Hill.

For those who wished to walk to Port Gaverne, a signpost at the three-way junction declared that that happy spot was all of a quarter of a mile away. Charlie rarely walked that far, although he was known to be not averse to strolling a little way out along New Road to visit the bar of the Lawns Hotel on the adjoining Terrace, overlooking Port Gaverne.

Charlie's visits to the Lawns bar were impeccably timed to commence a few minutes before closing time. This narrow window of opportunity permitted Charlie not only to be stood a round by the unwary, but also to be relieved of having to respond with a round of his own through the welcome (to Charlie) cry by George Moth, the genial landlord, of "Time gentlemen, please!"

———

Charlie's conglomeration of garages was extensive enough to press on back from New Road to be halted only by the rear wall of the New Coastguard Station. From the front of the New Coastguard Station it then only needed a few hops, skips and jumps and one careless stumble to reach the edge of the cliffs.

The nerve centre of Charlie's garage empire was a vehicle service and repair shop that opened a sliding front entry on to New Road. In the isosceles triangle contained by the roof and the top of the sliding front was set the grand title "North Cornwall Transport", painted in large block capitals. "Co. Ltd." was added in smaller capitals, probably as an afterthought, since the "Ltd." pushed the availability of space to a dangerous limit.

The North Cornwall Transport service shop was a barn of barely penetrable gloom in which, to judge from the state of the floor, copious amounts of oil had been spilled and left to seep and stagnate over an extended period of time. In the centre of the crusted floor an inspection pit loomed like an open grave from which anything could emerge and one day very possibly would.

———

Within the dim interior, Bert Keat, Charlie's right hand man and incidental mechanic, was a grizzled presence who picked his constant way over discarded spare parts and around and under sad cars resigned to the knowledge that they might be attended to dreckly.

Bert walked with a pronounced limp, the casualty of a car backfiring against his right leg. Bert was never going to give a frustrated car the opportunity to do that to him again, so Bert, and the garaged cars, were all tending to bide their time.

———

As important as were the facilities of North Cornwall Transport's car service shop, not excepting the petrol-dispensing pumps that stood on a raised platform to its left, it was a former garage at the rear of Charlie's complex near the New Coastguard Station that was the jewel in Charlie's crown. Few people living in Port Isaac would have argued otherwise.

Charlie converted this former garage into a public entertainment institution that hosted a weekly cinema performance, and which was an incidental venue for dances, concerts and a range of not always appropriately named talent competitions. The institution was not only famed, it was legendary. It exulted in its name, the Rivoli.

———

The Rivoli also found strength in its very own resident musical trio, which provided the accompaniment for dances, and naturally enough named itself the "Rivolians".

The members of the trio were Mr and Mrs Cecil Brimbacombe (on violin and drums respectively) and Mrs Boss Richards (on piano). Mrs Boss played the Rivoli piano with all the assurance of one who knew she was about to lose the contest.

Cecil, best known as "Brimmy", had something of the look of an overweight Buffalo Bill, best typified in his flowing silver locks and a similarly toned goatee beard trimmed sharply enough to spear an apple on its point. Brimmy was an accomplished musician, well able to coax sweet melodies from his favoured instrument. It was just something of a pity that he had to battle through the dance numbers against both Mrs Brimmy's single-minded determination to beat her drums into submission and Mrs Boss's faltering attacks on discord.

Mrs Brimmy was much taller than Brimmy. She resembled a gaunt Edith Sitwell, as if Edith was not gaunt enough in her own right. The cast of Mrs Brimmy's mouth was disapproving enough to be the envy of any regular chapelgoer. She could generate any kind of strict dance tempo on the drums and had a particular expertise in converting them all to waltzes.

⸺

The Rivoli was cement-floored, consistent with its former life as one of Charlie's garages. The inspection pit, if it had ever existed, was filled in. Oil stains had somehow been banished, perhaps by magic.

The walls and roof of the Rivoli were made of corrugated metal sheets. It didn't require a particularly heavy shower of rain on the exterior of the building to effectively overwhelm any sound generated within, whether this emanated from the Rivolians or from the silver screen (or, for those who were not interested in euphemisms, from the white bedsheet screen drawn tight at the back of the small trestle-mounted wooden stage on which the Rivolians performed).

Cement and corrugated metal combined to guarantee that inside the hallowed auditorium of the Rivoli, no matter how many bodies were packed together, and whatever the season of the year, chill crept around the walls and reigned supreme on the floor.

Dances in the Rivoli were held mainly in the summer months. A pressing problem calling for resolution was that the concrete floor was resistant to the soles of shoes, and the friction thereby generated made it a near impossibility for feet to keep time with the music on the occasions that the Rivolians' music actually was in time.

The liberal use of ballroom chalk on the cement floor – intended to permit dancers to glide like Fred Astaire and Ginger Rogers, whose exploits on the Rivoli screen were exceedingly popular with patrons – served to turn the floor into a respectable imitation of an ice rink. Dancing feet shot off in unintended directions, placing their owners in positions incompatible with the kind of dance floor decorum of which Victor Sylvester might have approved, but which was quite the stuff of life to the Rivolians.

For cinema performances the Rivoli boasted several rows of "shilling" seats, many of which, prior to their salvage from a once opulent cinema fallen on hard times, might have seen better days, but had never provided more illustrious service to cinemagoers' backsides than they did at the Rivoli.

The shilling seats tilted back when their occupants stood up. The seats were covered in faded threadbare blue plush. Dust puffed around every backside lowered onto one of them. When dances were held, the rows of shilling seats were removed to make space and stored at the rear of the Rivoli.

Since cinema at the Rivoli was a weekly event of such signifi-cance to its patrons, more than a few of the shilling seats were regularly spoken for. There were few third-party crimes more heinous than occupying a specific shilling seat – inadvertently or deliberately, it made no difference – that belonged to a patron who had assumed proprietary rights as a Rivoli regular.

—

Mrs Charlie Lobb's father, Mr Roseveare, lived with his daughter and Charlie in their cottage on Back Hill. Mr Roseveare was known as "Rosie". He was a moderately heavily set gentleman, slow moving on account of his advancing age. The remaining hair that adhered to Rosie's head was so white and finely drawn that he appeared to be as good as bald. A fiercely clipped moustache on Rosie's upper lip provided evidence however that all was not yet lost.

Rosie's nickname was, for most of the time, a good fit with his general temperament. He was tireless in his support for St Peter's church, and made an excellent master of ceremonies at many church functions, most famous among which was the annual auction of produce donated to the church Harvest Festival. Audiences rose to Rosie's sympathetic patter and great good humour.

However, Rosie had another side to his character, reserved exclusively for the boys who patronised the Rivoli with a dedication that would have wrought marvels had it been applied by them to school subjects. Charlie employed Rosie as the Rivoli usher, and the prime responsibility of the Rivoli usher, as Rosie saw it, was to eject boys from cinema performances whenever the least vestige of an opportunity presented itself.

Under Rosie's uncompromising efforts against the boys' self-asserted interests, a game developed in which all those playing knew their respective roles and played them out to the bitter end.

—

In front of the dusty shilling seats at the Rivoli were set a few ranks of wooden benches. The benches were long, hard, rustic in style and devoid of back support. They were the "sixpenny seats".

All the boys sat on the sixpennies, where, prior to the lights going down as the cinema performance commenced, and under Rosie's all-encompassing eyes, they were obliged to maintain a modest reserve. Rosie threw few boys out of the Rivoli before the performance began as there would be no fun for him in that. He was, however, never unwilling to pounce when least expected.

—

The entrance to the Rivoli was "U" shaped, bent around a central corrugated metal sheet. This contrivance reduced the capacity of light to penetrate the Rivoli on summer evenings. Immediately inside the entry Rosie maintained a vigilant presence.

Miss Lillian Roseveare, Rosie's daughter, was seated at a small card table alongside Rosie. Lillian took the entry fees and in return issued perforated tickets which she pulled away from a broad flat roll. Rosie then tore the tickets in half to validate them. He retained one half of the ticket and handed the other half to the patron who had just paid for it.

Patrons took their seats to the accompaniment of recorded music played on a gramophone. If the sequence of this music ever varied, none of the boys was aware of it. They reasoned that Charlie had inherited a few everlasting 78-rpm records and was therefore uninterested in extending the range. Rosie and cinema at the Rivoli were to be forever linked to Mantovani's cascading strings arrangement of "Charmaine".

—

Although Charlie owned the Rivoli, the projection equipment was the property of Mr Oliver from St Teath. Mr Oliver managed an itinerant cinema, taking films, shorts and serials around North Cornwall, making a stop at a different village each night. He came to the Port Isaac Rivoli on Fridays. The narrow posters that Mr Oliver put up around Port Isaac in advance of his visits, headed "Cinema at the Rivoli" and advertising coming attractions, were awaited by patrons with unsuppressed eagerness.

A standard evening at the Rivoli cinema usually consisted of a "big film" accompanied by a "full supporting programme". The latter comprised a cartoon, a travelogue, or perhaps a *Pete Smith Speciality* or a *Crime Does Not Pay* feature. Sometimes, although not often, two long films might be shown consecutively, in which case the second one would be the "big film" and the first one the "little film". Most popular of all with the boys were cliffhanger serials like *The Clutching Hand* and *Flash Gordon* – or, as Ming the Merciless pronounced it, "Flaish Gordon".

The boys were invariably on their best behaviour before and during the showing of the latest episode of a serial, as it would have been disastrous for them to miss it owing to being thrown out of the Rivoli by Rosie. The serials were acted out and embellished in the games the boys played through the succeeding week, as were also some of the subjects of the big films themselves when these involved cowboys and Indians, swordplay of any kind, or Johnny Weismuller starring as Tarzan.

Mr Oliver's equipment was serviceable, but temporary suspensions of service through mechanical failure, a sudden unscheduled split in the continuity of the film, a change of reel, or reels shown out of sequence were not uncommon. Such blackout events provided a trigger for a cacophony of whistling and yelling to break out from the sixpennies.

A similar level of justifiable protest from the sixpennies was also retained for high boredom quotient big film dramas, as well as for romantic scenes in what the boys referred to with contempt as "kissing films".

Moved by the outraged expression from the sixpennies, Rosie, for all the world like Blind Pew on his way to the Admiral Benbow, plodded in their direction through the darkness, his hands seeking a purchase on the first jersey or coat that he could get hold of. The boys rolled on the floor under the wooden benches, or scuttled back for cover towards the shilling seats. Rosie never entered the exalted realm of the shilling seats.

It was not that it mattered, as Rosie always got hold of one of the boys. Protestations of innocence served for nothing with Rosie, and his captive was ceremoniously slung from the Rivoli into the night through the galvanised sheet entry.

Having made a kill, Rosie's hunting instincts were satisfied for a while. The boys remaining in the sixpennies were then comparatively safe until the next overlong screen kiss or problem with Mr Oliver's projector gave rise to their customary foot stamping, whistling and barracking and set the game with Rosie in progress once more.

Port Isaac viewed from half way up Church Hill

5

Doctor

AT THE VERY BOTTOM of Trewetha Lane, on its curling lower corner with Back Hill and set upon a high bank behind a crest of feathery tamarisk bushes, stood the home and surgery of Dr Donald McDougall Sproull.

Dr Sproull was not merely a general practitioner of medicine, he was also a family counsellor and committed friend to the population of Port Isaac in sickness and in health till death did them part.

Across the way, on the redoubt opposite Dr Sproull's residence and standing at about the same elevation above Back Hill, the grey bulk of St Peter's church strove to maintain a rival pride of place, and in an occasional good light might even have managed to give the impression that it was on the point of succeeding.

The bank surmounted by Dr Sproull's house was as steep as it was high. A geologist might have observed that the bank was underlain by slate in an advanced state of weather-induced deterioration. The surface of the slate flaked, dribbled, peeled and crumbled to fine powder at the least touch of a hand or foot. The bank thwarted even the most determined attempt to be climbed, as much in dry weather as when it was wet and the rain turned the dust to greasy clay as slippery as lard.

It was perhaps fortunate that a running assault on the bank was not the only way to gain access to Dr Sproull's house and surgery.

45

Only a short step up along Trewetha Lane from the Back Hill corner, an entrance wide enough for a lorry to drive through, that gave onto a gravelled yard big enough for several lorries to park in, brought visitors into a position to contemplate Dr Sproull's front door directly. But it was much more likely that opening the surgery door would form their primary objective.

Dr Sproull's house was a large rambling building, mansion-like by Port Isaac standards. His surgery, a meeting place as much for the sound of mind and body as for the halt of limb and constitution, was located just inside the entry from Trewetha Lane. The surgery was appended to the side of the house as if it was a squat afterthought.

———

Dr Sproull was not from Port Isaac. He was not, for that matter, from Cornwall either. He was Scottish to the core of his being, and was imbued with all the dour, down to earth bluntness and pragmatism for which the Scottish race was justifiably renowned, particularly on flag days. These were essential attributes for a GP practising in a village like Port Isaac, where hypochondria and malingering were nothing if not endemic, and in which life was directed by principles that were not always unparsimonious.

If Dr Sproull had little time to spare for malingerers, he had even less time to offer to those whose political persuasion favoured the Conservative party. He leaned precariously to the political left, and was unequivocally on the side of all social underdogs. Church and chapel were one of a kind to him and he treated them both as such without fear or favour. He brooked no humbug from man or beast, while being the very soul of discretion. Dourness was a cloak he wore to cover an intensely caring heart.

No call for help came too late in the day or night to count on Dr Sproull's immediate attention. No cottage in the parish was too humble or too remotely located for Dr Sproull to visit when he was needed; no weather was too inclement to halt his regular rounds. The comfort, reassurance and well being of his patients were both Dr Sproull's clear motivation and his overriding priority.

All his patients knew him as "Doctor", the name being applied not in the sense of due title, although of course it was that, but rather as a term of affection, as if it were a nickname or an endearment. "Doctor" gave due acknowledgement to the feeling that Dr Sproull was someone extraordinarily special.

———

Doctor maintained a keen interest in the welfare of every Port Isaac child he brought into the world, and there were many of them. He remembered their birthdays, and took as much pride in their achievements (and perhaps a great deal more in some cases) as did the same children's parents.

Anyone who passed the eleven plus grammar school examination could do so with the assurance of being the beneficiary of a one pound note from Doctor. Whether it was crisp or limp, a pound note was a pound note. Those who made it onwards through the school certificate examinations to gain university entry were destined to be the even luckier recipients of a cheque written out in Doctor's own hand for the sum of five pounds.

———

James was one such boy for whom a cheque from Doctor for five pounds arrived one day in the post. The value of the cheque represented more money in James's own name that he had ever held in his hands before. It was also the first cheque he had ever seen, let alone touched.

Fate might have conspired to allow James to accede to university entry, but he had no idea what he needed to do with a cheque to turn it into real money. Nor for that matter did anyone else in his family. Owners of bank accounts in Port Isaac were few and far between, even assuming that they were endowed with sufficient funds to open an account in the first place. Those who had any money at all preferred to keep their cash where they could both see and touch it.

James was advised to take Doctor's cheque up to the Co-op

shop on the crest of New Road, there to enquire if it could be converted into cash. Both his mother and his grandmother were members of the Co-operative Wholesale Society with individual membership numbers (654 and 1137 respectively) against which their "divvy" was reckoned, so his chances of success in cashing the cheque at the Co-op were reckoned to be reasonable.

The Co-op manager at the time was Mr Freddy Angove. Freddy succeeded the former manager Mr Auger, an imposing martinet who bore a striking resemblance to the fine character actor Raymond Huntley.

Freddy, who was not obviously blessed with the type of urbane disposition that Raymond epitomised, left James standing like a supplicant at the marbled Co-op grocery counter while he demonstrated his managerial importance by waving Doctor's cheque around in the air for the benefit of a backing chorus of simpering customers.

Freddy ordered James to return home to obtain written authorisation from his mother for the cheque-cashing transaction. He laughed cynically at James when James returned in the hope of completing the transaction for not knowing what "endorsement" meant, and then, when James found out what it did mean, for not knowing how to apply the required action to the back of a cheque.

Mr Freddy Angove humiliated James in a manner that was cheap and unnecessary, but not unique in the annals of Port Isaac men's behaviour to boys. It was only to be expected really, and was there to be endured in order to be able to move on.

———

After the days of Doctor's incumbency in Port Isaac, successive members of the medical profession practised locally, some perhaps with as much skill as Doctor, but none with greater effect on patient's hearts and minds. Those who followed Doctor were doctors, but there was and would ever be only one Doctor.

———

Doctor wore his hair unfashionably long. It fell in waves to each side of his head from a central parting and was held in place by the earpieces of his glasses, which tucked it neatly out of the way behind his ears. Any length of hair exceeding the classic "short back and sides and some off the top" style of the Port Isaac barber, Mr William John Honey, was held to be within the remit of intellectuals, of whom there were precious few in Port Isaac.

Doctor's head was poised slightly forward, as if he was balancing a heavier than usual weight on his shoulders. His lips were full but they were not pendulous. There was a touch of Winston Churchill in his features as well as in the way he bore himself, although given Doctor's political persuasion, any parallel with Mr Churchill was not one that he would have welcomed.

———

James's Gran Creighton and his mother Betty both carried out domestic service for Doctor and his wife Winifred, and in the process developed a regard for Doctor that was appreciably close to hero worship. Doctor's socialist outlook might have been set in some form of concrete, but there were limits after all, and when status required service, then service it was.

Any misgivings felt by Betty and Gran Creighton during their long association with Doctor and Mrs Sproull related only to Doctor's political tendencies. Betty was once shocked to discover that he not only subscribed to the exceedingly left-leaning periodical *New Statesman* but was prone to leave copies of this offensive item lying around so openly in his house that the corruption of unwary visitors by it was almost unavoidable.

Port Isaac was a political stronghold of the Liberal party. It always had been, and as far as people like Betty were concerned, it always would be because it always had been. Liberalism was rooted so deeply in tradition that all sense of objectivity about the reason why had long since taken flight. It was invariably judged by Port Isaac people that what was good enough for their forefathers to vote for was quite good enough for them.

The Labour party was to all intents and purposes either unknown or otherwise unwanted in Port Isaac. The Conservatives had a certain number of adherents who supported their cause, but their grip on local political life was tenuous. Conservatives were, as often as not, stamped with the smugness of privilege, and were unquestioningly regarded as "betters".

In Betty's view, danger lay in anyone touching such a publication as the *New Statesman*, let alone in reading it, assuming, that is, that those who touched it could read. Betty could never bring herself to pick up the *New Statesman* from where Doctor had discarded it.

The one saving grace for Betty perhaps was that the *New Statesman* had not yet found its way into the waiting room of the surgery.

———

Doctor's social conscience achieved its finest hour in the Lobber field affair.

The back hedge of Lobber field was very old. It lost itself in thick gorse towards the crest of Lobber cliff, up above the western breakwater and just past the broad opening where the footpath to the inlet known as Pine Awn passed through. This opening, a hallowed right of way, was discovered one morning to have been built up and closed off to public access by the farmer who owned the land.

It was an outrage that provoked much protest. The farmer could not be persuaded to reconsider his position, and the access remained blocked. Any farmer was pretty much by definition certain to be of landed gentry stock. Whatever the landed gentry and their ilk did had, again by convention, to be right and proper. Port Isaac people knew their place. Whether they liked it or not, the path closure had to be lumped.

Fortunately for the many who knew their place in Port Isaac society, Doctor loved to walk the path to Pine Awn as much as anyone. The far slope of Pine Awn was an unparalleled springtime spectacle of primroses and bluebells. Firm in his belief that authority had gone beyond an acceptable limit in denying the public its right of way, and correctly judging that his patients were people of many words and very few deeds, Doctor elected himself to be their standard bearer.

Doctor ascended Lobber field, approached the infamous blockage and personally tore it down, stone by stone, until the way through was clear. He followed up this feat of arms with a public declaration that should the wall be raised again, he would return to raze it once more, and would continue to do so if required until the injustice was corrected.

That ended the matter at a stroke. No farmer was ever going to be bold enough to do battle with Doctor. The way through the Lobber hedge, consequently christened "Doctor's Gap", remained open as a monument to Doctor's blessed action in the ultimate triumph of good over evil. Never in a conflict on Lobber field was so much done for so many as was done by one Doctor.

———

Doctor's outlook on life might well have been classless, but his social class undoubtedly ranked as far above that of the majority of his patients as it was above that of any stereotypically grimy necked, flat-capped Labour party adherent. Doctor was a consummate professional man. He travelled in a chauffeur-driven car, he had a telephone installed in his house, he wore a tie regularly, and last but by no means least his family ate a turkey at Christmas time.

A turkey, representing luxury of a kind that was so rare as to be barely imagined on most tables in Port Isaac, in or out of the Christmas season, placed a hallmark on Doctor's status as a man to be reckoned with.

Mrs Sproull gave Gran Creighton a few slices of turkey on one special Christmas day. It was the first encounter with turkey meat that Gran Creighton had had. Sad to say, Mrs Sproull's largesse provided a lesson of discovery that the truth did not live up to the myth. Gran Creighton and Betty adjudged the turkey meat to be too dry and equally devoid of flavour to have real merit. However, few crumbs of poultry from a benefactor's table were ever received with more delight when they were handed over on that memorable occasion.

————

Doctor's surgery was open every night of the week and closed only on Sundays. The surgery door opened directly into a small waiting room, which was brightly decorated and always welcoming during any season of the year. A cosy fire was a regular feature in the fireplace once the autumn arrived and the evenings began to draw in. A heavy door to the left of the fireplace led into Doctor's office and consulting room, an inner sanctum of dark wood, gleaming glass and polished leather.

Straight-backed chairs were lined up around the walls of the waiting room. The chairs were always occupied during the hours when the surgery was open. A small proportion of those seated might have genuinely come along to the surgery to consult Doctor, although if they had they were in the minority.

Dialogue between the genuine and the would-be patients and the unashamedly non-patients in Doctor's surgery waiting-room revolved almost exclusively around the recounting of respective medical histories with the confirmed intent of the one to outdo the other. A medical complaint announced by one patient was sure to be immediately trumped by a second, allegedly more serious (and preferably more life-threatening), complaint by another.

All those present wallowed self-indulgently in a warm bath of shared misfortune, and were much happier for the experience. Much of the information gleaned was destined, with suitable elaboration, to be passed on to chance met and specifically sought out acquaintances on the morrow.

Solid though the door to Doctor's office was, and muted though his "bedside manner" tone of voice might have been within his office, the confidentiality of medical consultation was constantly being challenged by the questing ears of those seated in the waiting room, who had invested a lifetime in perfecting the art of eavesdropping.

—

Doctor's diagnostic technique was formidably direct. Faced with a patient complaining of an ache or a pain, his first action was to vigorously probe and manipulate the allegedly affected part of the body, while querying if it hurt at all. The patient's reaction, as measured by the volume and duration of the ensuing anguished scream, which rendered Doctor's question redundant, was considered by Doctor to be directly proportional to the seriousness of the ailment.

—

On the mantlepiece above the surgery waiting-room fireplace, flat-fronted bottles and squat jars of medicinal remedies that Doctor had prescribed, and in many cases mixed with his own hands, stood in a proud row waiting for collection. The bottles were cork-stoppered and clearly labelled with the recipient's name and the recommended daily dosage to be taken.

The contained liquids were coloured pink, white, orange and brown. Many of them tasted unpleasant, but as far as the patients were concerned the worse the taste the more effective the remedy was likely to be.

Some of the bottled draughts were thick and opaque in appearance, and others were light and clear. Some may have had an authentic medicinal content, and some may not, although they all seemed to work as the patients kept returning for more.

Pawlyn's cellars and the upper Town Platt, Port Isaac

6

The Fishermen's Beat

AT SUCH TIMES AS it was deemed essential, any fishing boat might be hauled all the way up from its mooring position onto the Town Platt for painting or repairs, or even, perish that thought as it smacked of work, for a touch of maintenance.

Any incidence of clumping barnacles on the lower hull of a fishing boat was generally rare, although attachments of parasitic strings of festooning seaweed were common enough. It was not necessary to move a fishing boat up to the Town Platt for such exotic growths to be removed from the hull, as the fishermen were well able to scrape seaweed away when the fishing boats lay marooned on the sand at low tide.

The upper edge of the Town Platt was raised a single step up above the tail end of Fore Street, which it bordered. In its association with Fore Street the Town Platt was appreciably flat-surfaced, but that planar situation didn't endure for long as the said surface quickly dropped away in a lengthy slope falling down to the top of the harbour beach.

Small wooden, clinker-built punts, the identically painted offspring of their parent fishing boats, made their customary home on the downward slope of the Town Platt, other than when the big tides and ground seas surged up onto, and not infrequently over, the slope. Then the punts were taken along Middle Street until the falling tide signified that the emergency was over. The scattered arrangement of the punts on the Town Platt might have looked not a little haphazard to a casual observer, most probably because it was.

——

Assuming the availability of sufficient hands, some willing, others impressed into willingness, punts were relatively easy to manœuvre up and down between the Town Platt and wherever the lapping edge of the tide happened to be at the time. The important function of a punt was to conduct its fishing boat crew in comparative safety to and from the shoreline and the fishing boat floating at its moorings.

Punts were propelled around the harbour by an action known as "sculling". This involved employing a single oar worked in a figure-of-eight motion across a stern-mounted rowlock. An experienced sculler was able to propel a punt with a seemingly effortless one-handed wrist action that caused the blade of the oar to bite hard at the yielding sea. The punt slipped along as smoothly as the lie of cream on scalded milk.

——

In the days before an auxiliary winch was set up at the top of the Town Platt adjacent to the step down into Fore Street, fishing boats were manually hauled up the beach to the Town Platt with the help of a set of half a dozen or more portable rollers. The fishing boats were not of especially large dimension but were heavy enough to ensure an onerous element in the progress of their movement.

A roller comprised a single cylindrical iron idler, worn down by age and application, not unlike some of the Port Isaac fishermen. The roller was mounted on an inadequately greased axle set in a much-abused wooden frame. As a fishing boat was pulled over the rollers in the direction of the Town Platt, the roller at the rear was lifted and carried forward as the stern end of the keel cleared it, and was then dropped in line ahead of the bow.

Those who were delegated to move the rollers had to work expeditiously, since a fishing boat, once it was in motion on the rollers, assumed a life of its own in sustaining forward momentum. Much unhappiness was generated among the fishermen when there was not a roller in place to meet the advancing bow. The fishermen were not farmers, and were easily disenchanted with ploughing sand.

When they were standing on the Town Platt, fishing boats and their punts were held in an upright position by wooden right-angled triangular frames, known as "trigs". One trig was firmly kicked into place against the hull on each side. A pair of trigs, in principle large open wedges, secured the fishing boats in a tightly rigid grasp.

<hr>

When it was commissioned, the Town Platt winch was equipped with a steel cable long enough to run out all the way down to the eastern breakwater. Operating the winch required a mighty handle, mounted on the right hand side, to be laboriously cranked round and round. Ostensibly to protect the winch mechanism against the weather, but just as probably to prevent any boys playing around with its handle, the machine was confined under a green wooden cover when not in official use.

The wooden cover looked like a second-rate carpenter's failed attempt to manufacture a cheap vaulting horse. However, it provided a most useful platform on which those members of Port Isaac society, for whom work was something that someone else did, could come to squat on their shiny trouser backsides or lean on threadbare jacketed elbows to soak up the sun and partake of incidental gossip. There they were able to contemplate the view of the harbour and to add their personal contribution to the greasy patina that always went hand in hand on surfaces that counted on the closely leaning attention of the sincerely idle.

<hr>

An inclined gully, floored with huge cobbles, ran deep down to the beach on the left hand side of the Town Platt. This was the lifeboat slipway, although for some time there had been no resident lifeboat in Port Isaac to slip its way along the course. The lifeboat, a former Port Isaac institution, had been relocated to the port of Padstow sometime before the war. This was a loss to Port Isaac tradition that was keenly felt. The Port Isaac lifeboat crew were held sacred in memory as having been men among men.

On the far left hand side of the lifeboat slipway the dark slate-built wall of Pawlyn's fish cellars rose like a would-be cliff. The wall was devoid of any features other than a couple of tight ventilation slits through which an arrow could just about be fired if necessary. Whether fired in anger or in jest, all that mattered was that someone might decide to have a go sometime. Sad to say, no one ever did.

Pawlyn's cellars were familiarly referred to as "Pawlyn's", and were not unnaturally owned by the Pawlyn brothers, who hailed from Padstow, as far as was known. Pawlyn's could be located just as well by smell as by sight, especially on a foggy day.

———

Channelled between Pawlyn's Lakeside wall and the left hand rim of the lifeboat slipway, the Lake, the final extension of the stream that had begun life up at Colstanton and Tresungers in the far recesses of the Port Isaac valley, was getting ready to spend itself and its cargo on the harbour beach.

In its passage through lower Port Isaac the Lake more or less followed the line of Middle Street through a narrowly contained slate-walled channel and a succession of mysterious tunnels in which creeping rats dragged their damp tracked tails.

Residents of downtown Port Isaac, few of whose cottages were associated with plumbing of either the indoor or the outdoor variety, took great comfort in the ready ability of the Lake to carry away in its cleansing flow a wide range of items of household waste, not forgetting the early morning contents of enamel buckets and china pos.

About half way up along Middle Street towards the Wesley Chapel, at the place where the Lake passed between Mr Tom

58

Saundry's greengrocery shop and the sidewall of Worden's butcher's shop, the Lake was fitted with a wooden flush gate. Operating the flush was one of the regular duties of the Port Isaac street cleaner, Mr Ned Cowlyn.

Every once in a while old Ned shuffled along to close the flush gate so as to build a great upstream head of water. Once he judged that he had a sufficient head in place, Ned released the flush gate, and the pent up water surged in a mighty wave along the Lake all the way down to the beach, carrying all it met before it.

Groups of boys gathered outside Tom Saundry's shop to watch the head of water rise to the limit allotted it by Ned, and then, when Ned let the water go, they tried, with occasional success, to race the flush wave to the slipway by way of Middle Street.

The flush wave, crested among other items of interest with potato peelings, tea leaves, rotten cabbage, shit, drowned kittens, edges of pastry that were once too hard but were too hard no longer, and mildewing bread, surged onto the beach and died. As it expired, it became the immediate focus of an almighty host of screaming gulls, none of which gave any quarter in scrabbling and squabbling for every succulent fragment of newly arrived largesse, until the beach was picked as clean as a mutton bone.

———

On the left hand side at the head of the slipway a flight of deeply worn slate steps, protected on the outside by a wooden handrail of equal antiquity, led from street level up to the upper floor of Pawlyn's. At the top of the steps a paint-peeling entry door opened into a room used as an office both by the Port Isaac Harbourmaster, Mr Anthony Provis, and the manager of Pawlyn's, Mr Tom Brown.

Tom was a voracious reader of western yarns. Equipped with a desert-dry wit, he made as laconic and rangy a figure as any cowhand he ever read about. He was the eldest of a large generation of a distinguished Port Isaac family line. Tom had five brothers, Carveth (known as "Veth"), Edwin ("Tinker"), Frank

("Nibs"), Bill ("Pink") and George. The family must have run out of nicknames by the time George, the youngest, was born. There was one sister, Winifred ("Winnie"), after whom the family's fishing boat, the biggest in the harbour, was named.

Anthony and Tom dodged up and down the steps and in and out of their office door, adopting a busy air that did little to hide the impression that they preferred to be on the outside rather than on the inside. From the little balcony-like area at the top of the steps, Anthony could inspect his entire harbour with a commanding glance, noting, not without hope, that the acetylene light was still pulsing on the western breakwaters, and counting the fishing boats at their moorings to make sure they were still all there.

———

On entering Tom and Anthony's office, any sensation of observed exterior shabbiness was not reversed. The office contained a superannuated wooden table, more severely wounded than scarred, which would have been flattered to have had its top clad in the *News of the World*. Standing by the table were a couple of well-matched chairs that had no doubt fought themselves to a standstill in bare-knuckle days.

The office decor was completed by the presence here and there of a few yellowing documents, none of them obvious missives carrying any hint of urgency, and very few of them recently submitted via His Majesty's mail. At and around average shoulder height, the office walls bore a grimy sheen celebrating the enterprise of those whose bounden duty had been to ensure that those walls never lacked internal support.

From time to time, one or more of the harbourmaster's cronies might emerge from the office with a purposeful air and descend the steps on a vital errand to which he only was privy. Sometimes this would be to consult the barometer set into its glass-fronted cubby behind a little door on the Fore Street facing front of Pawlyn's.

———

Inside, Pawlyn's cellars were an establishment of rapidly hurrying activity. Fish, crabs and lobsters were delivered directly to the inner precincts of Pawlyn's from the fishing boats, carried by the fishermen, both ponderously and with no small sense of self-importance, up from the beach in the big two-handled woven withy pads.

Heavily driven seas on the fist of a high tide were apt to beat hard at the slipway cobbles and to claw aggressively at Pawlyn's outer wall with a single-minded determination to recover, dead or alive, any fish held captive inside Pawlyn's.

Within Pawlyn's the catches were weighed and packed tight in wooden crates marked with the stencil "Pawlyn Bros". The crated fish were covered with very coarse crystalline salt before the crates were closed for transport out of Port Isaac by lorry. Crabs and lobsters were crated alive, buried under dry sawdust.

———

Tom Brown explained to the curious boys the reason for packing crabs and lobsters in a medium as unusual as sawdust. Tom told the boys that the objective was to ensure a self-sustaining venture.

"The buggers eat up the sawdust and shit planks. The planks get sawed up to make more crates to ship out the next lot, and the sawdust from sawing up the planks is used for the next packing".

All that was necessary to keep the process going was to get hold of some nails. The boys were sure that Tom was working on a way to feed the crabs and lobsters with iron filings, or something like that, so they could shit planks with the nails already in them.

———

The varieties of fish handled by Pawlyn's were seasonal, although some species, such as mackerel, were generally available throughout the year. In the late autumn and the early winter enormous catches of herrings were taken. The fishing boats often returned to the harbour laden to the gunwales and close to the point of sinking under an accumulated weight of herrings numbered in the hundreds of thousands. Large quantities of the herrings were kippered. Pawlyn's was fitted with a kipper house, and there was a whole bank of such kipper houses out at Port Gaverne over the hill to the east.

The herring catch was shaken out of the nets directly from the fishing boats on the beach at low tide. Scales flew far and wide, and lay in iridescent piles on the sand and rocks, thicker than confetti on Back Hill after a wedding at St Peter's church.

To the great misfortune of the Port Isaac fishing industry, the herring shoals deserted Port Isaac Bay not long after the war. The departure of the herrings was blamed, perhaps not without some justification, on the Royal Air Force. The RAF, which used the arm of Port Isaac Bay to the east of Port Gaverne as a range to practise bombing runs, made an excellent scapegoat for the disappearance of the herrings. Aircraft were seen making pass after pass across Port Isaac Bay either to shoot at, or to aim and drop smoke bombs on floating targets.

Discharged smoke bombs, some expired, some still very much alive, washed up regularly on the shoreline around the Port Isaac and Port Gaverne area. The bombs were made of a light metal painted yellow and were long, thin and cylindrical, with a tapered tail ending in a set of fins. For the boys, smoke bombs were always welcome finds. They hacked open the casings to induce the bombs in which life remained to continue to give up as much smoke as was still feasible.

Other species of fish brought into Port Isaac were cod, pollock, dogfish and gurnard, and flat fish like plaice and sole. Dogfish, with their abrasive brown mottled skin and shark-like appearance, were thrown onto the beach for the gulls to scavenge. No one ever ate a dogfish – well, no one admitted to eating a dogfish.

The gurnard was a streaky red, startled looking, big-mouthed fish referred to by those who dealt with it in Pawlyn's as "gurnet". Gurnet was used mainly for baiting withy-made crab pots. Individual gurnets were pinned securely to the inside base of crab pots by sharp hand-whittled wooden stakes named "skivvers".

The stock of dead gurnet destined for use as crab pot bait was stored, pending its retrieval, in a deep-sunken concrete tank on the Roscarrock Hill side of the near back corner of Pawlyn's. The odour around the gurnet tank was much more vibrant than the gurnet that generated it had probably ever been, and was suffused with enough ripeness of power to make a fisherman surrender to it, let alone a crab or a lobster.

———

There were two varieties of commercial crabs caught in Port Isaac Bay. The principal type was the much-prized flat-shelled and huge-clawed brown crab known as a "waiter". The other was the spiny ovoid-shelled spider crab, which, given its long thin claws and legs, was a much less desirable proposition as far as crab meat production was concerned. Just like dogfish, spider crabs generally made good beach pickings for gulls.

When waiters were caught, much care was essential on the part of whoever removed them from the pots to avoid contact with their ever-ready claws. Waiters were capable of crushing rocks in their claws. More than one careless fisherman had had the extremity of a finger taken off by the claws of a waiter.

The technique – a process known as "nicking" – that a fisherman employed to render a waiter harmless was to grasp it from behind and slit the tendons on its articulated upper claws with a sharp blade.

———

Every fisherman carried a single-bladed clasp knife, generally bone handled. The knife blades were honed so regularly on whetstones that whetting could be considered to have assumed an obsessive hobby status. As a consequence, all clasp knife blades were shaped into wicked razor-edged curves. The function of these clasp knives, always ready to hand, was not only to nick the claws of waiters but also to cut and trim withies, carve out skivvers and pare slices away from ripe sticks of chewing tobacco to compose a "chaw of baccy".

Tom Brown, when the boys demanded it of him, was always prepared to take his own clasp knife from his pocket, to open up the blade and read solemnly some words which he claimed were inscribed on the metal and which perhaps really were. "This knife of best Sheffield steel", Tom read, "is guaranteed to make a figgy duff tremble, and a leg of mutton jump off the table".

―――

A "figgy duff" was a boiled pudding of suet in its purest form, studded with raisins. In the absence of raisins, sultanas or currants were used as a substitute. The trick in making a proper figgy duff was to ensure lightness of texture, and not everyone could achieve this. There were figgy duffs made in Port Isaac for which those who were about to receive them were not truly thankful, recognising that such figgy duffs could have been employed to bomb Hitler. It took a fearsome knife like Tom's to make figgy duffs like those tremble.

―――

One section of Pawlyn's was devoted to the manufacture of crab pots, plaited and woven from newly cut withies on ingeniously designed frames. Most of the withies were cut and shouldered down from the big withy garden up in the Port Isaac valley mill pool. The withies were carried in bundles an arm span in circumference, bound about with tarry twine. Some contributions to the withy harvest were also received from a range of individual withy trees, thrusting their gnarled and bristling fists out of the corners of allotments.

Around the crab pot makers, the walls of Pawlyn's were hung with fishing nets, either ready and willing for herrings, or under repairs, or otherwise awaiting carriage to the Bark House in lower Dolphin Street for their annual barking in the big copper full of boiling tannin solution.

As the fishermen worked, their conversation flow was as laden with hyperbole as it was deficient in vocabulary. Relevance was only incidental to the discussions and tended to occur more by default than by intent.

———

Meanwhile, outside on the Town Platt, or alternatively on the part of Fore Street in front of Pawlyn's steps, other fishermen walked off customary miles in a close formation skirmish line without ever leaving the immediate vicinity. They plodded and swivelled to and fro on the beat in a slow and close order step as they conversed, smoked, chewed and spat by turns, as if intent on going somewhere, but bound together as one with the sole purpose of going nowhere. Some of them may even have dozed off on the tread. Their common motion was akin to that of a slow flock of starlings flooding across a winter sky, wheeling backwards and forwards in instinctive unison.

———

Given that waiters and lobsters were such prolific residents of Port Isaac Bay, it seemed illogical that eating the creatures was a rather exclusive practice. Shellfish were, however, an expensive commodity, affordable only by the likes of those who didn't sound their "r"s when they spoke through what seemed to be a mouthful of damson stones.

This did not mean that occasional crabs did not fall into the hands of the likes of the Port Isaac born, who were devoted to the articulation of the letter "r" in all its rounded glory, it was just that they didn't fall thus very often. Lobsters for their part had essentially no dinner table association at all in Port Isaac cottages, but this didn't matter much as crabmeat, in the opinion of those who lived in the cottages, was superior to that of lobster in every way.

A crab handed over as a gift was not altogether unheard of, but since most Port Isaac fishermen adhered to the well-known adage that it was better to receive than give, living in the hope of fishermen's bounty was a lost cause. Clandestine acquisition of shellfish was another option, not that anyone ever took that route – well, not often anyway.

——

The process of boiling up, picking and dressing a crab was intricate. It called for a combination of patience and expertise that few possessed in optimum proportions. Those who had it found their services in huge demand in the summer by Terrace hoteliers anxious to assure the availability of dressed crab meat on their bill of fare, to be served up with a wilted lettuce leaf, a slice of tomato, and a boiled potato stuck over on the side.

Crabs met their fate by being dropped alive into boiling water. There was no real expertise required for that. It was claimed by some that they heard the crabs scream at the moment of immersion. It wouldn't have been a surprise if this were true.

The crab picker's skill came in dissembling the carcass of a cooked crab into its constituent parts, in knowing where to go into the anatomy to locate the meat, in gently cracking the claws and legs and winkling out every last shred of flesh, and in avoiding the inclusion of any fragments of shell in the finally dressed mass. Expectant visitors in hotel dining rooms would not be content to bite down on fragments of crab shell.

Dressed crab was presented in the crab's back shell, with the real or "white" meat mounded in the centre, and a revolting brown paste (the so called "brown meat"), framing the white meat on either side. The brown meat was extracted from the body of the crab behind the claw sockets. A true Port Isaac boy would not have eaten brown meat, even if it were to be offered free of charge.

The boys' delight was in white crabmeat seasoned with pepper and malt vinegar and placed between two slabs of Sherratt's new bread. A sandwich like that didn't come along very often, so that when one did it was savoured slowly, to sustain its memory until the next time.

——

A small portion of hotel-commissioned white crabmeat generally failed to escape from the cottage within which it had been extracted from its carapace, but as to where this white meat ended up, there was not one of those who picked it out who was ever going to be willing to say.

The rocks behind the eastern breakwater

7

The Ebb Tide

THE TIDE ALWAYS HAD, and as far as the Port Isaac boys knew always would, recede right out of the harbour and then move right back in again. It rose and fell pretty much a couple of times every day in a sort of erratic pattern of time that made an irritatingly moveable feast of the boys' plans to get out onto the rocks behind the eastern breakwater.

Robert Burns was good enough to advise all those who had read his poem "Tam O'Shanter" that "Nae man can tether time nor tide". Not that the boys were in any way familiar with Burns, but his comment was excellent counsel that nae man venturing behind either of the two harbour breakwaters at low tide should ever ignore, since the period of hiatus at low tide when tethering might just have been a reality was not of long duration.

Given that neither time nor tide waited for any man, there was just nae chance that either commodity would deign to wait for any boy. The best the boys could do was to seize what the day brought, if the day's conditions permitted them to.

Two additional variables that the boys needed to take into account in planning their over-the-breakwater forays were exactly how far and how fast the tide was prepared to climb up the beach before it called a halt to its advance, and on the opposite side of the coin how far down the beach and for how long the tide would sink before deciding that enough was enough.

The most treacherous kind of tide to race into the harbour was a "ground sea". The tormented soul of a ground sea was well hidden under its surface. Below the greasy cap of the ocean, ground-sea water was tainted an evil brownish grey, riotous with churning sand.

A ground sea swelled like a monster's back and advanced its deceptively shallow front with the pace of an express train, fast and furious. A ground sea could surge a hundred feet up the beach in one dash and then, as if it had never been, suck right back down again to where it had come from. Anyone who loitered too long on the beach had to make absolutely sure they were able to get out of the way when a ground sea came at them, as a ground sea in full flight could not be outdistanced and took no prisoners.

The surge of a ground sea was known as "the run". The run could generate a depth of five or six feet of voracious water over a place where there had been damp sand or shingle to stand on only seconds previously.

Roger Keat was caught by such a run of ground sea in front of the cave that pierced in under Roscarrock Hill on the downside of the pseudo-lookout tower attached to Halwyn house. There were many caves all around the harbour, some of them running away back into dreadful darkness. The boys called the caves "gugs".

Roger, in the path of the run, scrambled to the top of a prominent rib of rock that rose perhaps four feet above beach level near the Halwyn gug to wait for the ground sea to pass him, reach its anticipated limit and withdraw.

However if anticipation was one thing, real circumstances were another. The run just kept on coming and the turbulent sea continued rising up to and then over the top of the rock. It swamped and pulled at Roger's boots. There was a moment of panic, perhaps more on the part of the discomfited Roger than his somewhat gleeful companions who were well out of reach of the run.

The run hesitated for a moment, as if wondering whether

or not to proceed up Roger's legs, decided not to after all, and withdrew back down the beach, leaving Roger to climb off the rock and make his own run across the Lake in the direction of the security of the Town Platt as rapidly as possible.

———

Whenever the tide entered its not inappropriately named spring mode, one of its options was to ebb so far out that anyone could be forgiven for thinking that exposing Lobber Point in its entirety was the ultimate goal. The complementary option for a spring tide was to rise up and over the Town Platt and make its presence known in lower Middle Street. A high spring tide and a ground sea – now there was a fearful combination to contemplate.

At a wonderfully low state of spring tide, it was possible for the boys to take advantage of a most welcome opportunity to walk directly around the base of the outer face of the eastern breakwater and arrive in the Promised Land behind with feet allegedly as dry as those of Moses when he arrived on the far side of the Red Sea.

For just about any of the Port Isaac boys, such an opportunity was invariably considered to be too good to miss. Most of them favoured using the buttress-like ledge at the base of the eastern breakwater on which to make the circumnavigation, with one hand trailing the crusty wall of the breakwater and both feet testing the pitfall of the thick mat of slippery seaweed that graced the ledge.

The breakwater ledge was only about a foot and a half wide. Its height above the base of the breakwater, which was, at the lowest tide, a long stretch in excess of the height of an average boy, served to make the width feel even narrower and not a little precarious. The passage around the ledge seemed less hazardous when a certain depth of sea was available below to give the appearance that there was not so far to fall.

———

Some boys, under the duress of a dare, walked around the ledge when it was covered over with the water of a rising tide. Under those conditions they followed the ledge only to its mid-point at the back of the eastern breakwater, at which location a ladder way of stout iron rungs was built into a recess in the breakwater wall. The ladder way went all the way to the top of the breakwater and allowed the boys to climb up to safety.

The iron rungs were as round as apples. They were much too thick for boys to span their fingers all the way around. They were cased in with a hard deposit of cracking rust, made tough and all too solid thanks to a steady chemical reaction with the sea. For all that, the boys were happy to hang on the rungs either right way up or upside down, and to laugh at the thwarted sea down below them.

At the inner end of the harbour face of the eastern breakwater a shorter set of recessed iron rungs provided easier access to the breakwater top and the back route to the rocks behind. The boys raced at this ladder like sure-footed hares, down from the Town Platt into the harbour, then along by Long Pool and its contained array of storage pots crammed with lobsters and crabs, past the gug with the man made tunnel at its inner end leading in the direction of Mine Pit Corner, and up a slope of smooth rock, each boy anxious to be the first to grab the rungs and lead the way up and over the eastern breakwater.

———

The reasons for the boys going out behind the eastern breakwater were, simply put, because the tide was out, because it was there, and because they could.

From the top of the eastern breakwater there were three acceptable routes for a descent of the outer side. One route involved climbing down the long iron-runged ladder at the mid-point of the outer wall of the breakwater. A second route led off to the side on the right, along the cliff face. This was a route that the nimble feet of any boy could shimmer down. The third route was more directly up and over the eastern breakwater, requiring a couple of vertical drops on the outside of the breakwater to be negotiated. Since the third route was the most perilous of the three, it was always to be preferred over the other two.

––––

Once he was out behind the eastern breakwater any boy's immediate priority was to keep a watchful eye to the right and to be specifically alert for signs of activity at the top of the adjacent cliff in the location known to one and all as "Hillson's Dump".

That well employed dumping spot was named after Mr Hillson, farmer and Port Isaac milkman by profession. Mr Hillson walked his delivery route carrying a huge shiny bucket of creamy milk, so fresh from his cows as to be warm when he measured it out into his customers' enamelled basins, using a half-pint dipper. He lived in the last house out beyond Hillson's dump – a house as big and as weather beaten as Mr Hillson himself.

The relevant concern with being behind the eastern breakwater within range of Hillson's Dump was that there was an ever likely possibility that a load of some or other unwanted items might be heaved over the crest into the abyss beneath. Just what that load might consist of when it came cascading down was probably a matter that didn't really bear thinking about. Anything chucked out by a Port Isaac resident was absolutely certain to be devoid of quality, character and inherent capacity for any further use. If this were not so, it wouldn't have been discarded in the first place.

––––

Spread over the open area behind the eastern breakwater at low tide there was a crowded multitude of sea-smoothed loose rocks that, in the case of the more manageable ones at least, could be turned over so as to expose the forms of life rudely startled from their shelter beneath. The creatures found under these rocks counted some deeper water species among their numbers when compared to those that lived in the rocks around the beach in the comparative calm of the inner harbour.

Under the rocks outside the eastern breakwater lived strange velvet crabs, blue feathery crabs and more than a few baby waiters. If the latter ever survived to adulthood they would be candidates for the fishermen's crab pots.

Occasionally, stranded in a rock pool or lodged in a crack in the big rocks at the lower limit of the ebb tide there might be the chance to discover one of those more mature waiters, as the boys were told by someone who claimed to have not only found such a crab, but also to have caught it and taken it home to be cooked. The boys were never lucky enough to find big waiters, but it didn't stop them looking. The fact that they got nothing was looked at philosophically. Failure saved them from having to smuggle a waiter out of the harbour under the eyes of the ever-vigilant fishermen, who considered such bounty to be their property. Fishermen were not noted for magnanimity in defeat, not where boys were concerned for sure.

———

Many tiny crabs, ranging in diameter from pinhead to drawing pin head, scuttled wildly for cover whenever a rock was turned over. These were thought of as "Jesus" crabs by the more fervent Sunday school attendees among the smaller boys, acting under a shared illusion that Jesus would most definitely love anything as small and defenceless as those crabs.

Under the rocks the boys also found many of the little brown, blunt-headed fishes they called "moles". A mole was able to survive under a rock between tides on not much more than a skin of salt water.

Attached to the underside of some rocks were flaccid plots of red-brown and green sea anemones, and now and then a deeply autumnal red sucker-bellied fish, appropriately known as a "sticky rock", was spotted among them.

———

There were white whelks and iridescent winkles available under the rocks in droves, guarded as often as not by a lone hermit crab occupying a winkle shell. Once in a while the boys collected full pails of winkles to take home to be boiled up in a big saucepan and eaten with the addition of malt vinegar and pepper by those few who had patience enough to extract cooked winkle meat from the shells, one by one, with a pin.

The boys didn't want the whelks, and so, as Billy Cotton instructed them on the wireless almost every Sunday afternoon when *Family Favourites* was finished, they didn't "muck 'em abaht". *The Billy Cotton Band Show* was an after-dinner penance without which any boy's Sunday would never have been complete.

—

Once a few rocks had been rotated, and the crabs and fish beneath them had been adequately disturbed, the boys' attention turned to determining how far out along the edge of the open awn beyond the eastern breakwater they could prudently venture before being forced into retreat by the rising tide.

It was generally feasible for them to progress as far as the turn of the headland marking the eastern outer limit of the awn. Mr Hillson's house was then right up above the boys at the top of the cliff. The Kenewal rock sitting out in the awn, and Lobber Point marking the western outer limit, were over there on the sea-tossed left.

The Kenewal rock guarded the left hand side of a sandy-floored deep-water safe passage for fishing boats. It was equipped with sharp teeth in jaws that foamed with fury when they broke surface at low tide and snapped at the wind.

The boys usually called a halt to their advance beyond the eastern breakwater at the top rim of a rising shelf of rock. From there they could peer around the headland and follow the great sweep of Port Isaac Bay all the way up to Tintagel Head. A diagonal crack on the surface of the shelf allowed them to drag themselves up to its rim if, as it all too often did, the shelf bore a slick coat of green seaweed that was antipathetic to even the most hobnailed of boots.

The same crack also ran down the steep outer face of the shelf, and sometimes the boys climbed over the rim and down the face, using the crack for purchase. Mostly, however, they felt that climbing down wasn't worth the effort they would have to put into climbing back up again.

———

On the way out across the rocks, between the eastern breakwater and the goal of the final sloping shelf, the curl of the tide had carved out a selection of perfectly formed potholes. Some of the potholes were round, others were cylindrical, and a few were even conical. Each was a little sea-sculpted masterpiece in its own right.

In the manner of all treasure chests, this particular array of potholed gems was equipped with a crowning jewel. The prize was hidden from view behind a slight overhang in the rocks, located close to the foot of the cliffs about half way between the eastern breakwater and the final slippery shelf that the boys surmounted. It was a pool measuring about a yard across and a yard deep. The wall of the pool was coated from the water surface down in a flawless pale pink concretion, untrammelled by any form of seaweed.

This was "Pink Pool", as the boys called it. No trip made by them behind the eastern breakwater ever missed a visit to look down into the marvel of Pink Pool. It was there to be appreciated.

———

Close to Pink Pool, a short, narrow gug, in the professional hands of the tide, embodied all the technical characteristics of a jeweller's tumbling mill. In the inner sanctum of the gug only the hardest pebbles endured to be symmetrically ground and polished by the action of the sea into round, ovoid and elliptical perfection. Those who were happy to wade through the cold and slippery-bottomed pool protecting the entry to the little gug were able to make a personal selection from the banked-up works of pebbly art that were there displayed.

A couple of the boys were occasionally delegated to collect a few of the rounder pebbles for delivery to Mr Ted Robinson at his Harbour Café. Ted was a celebrated Port Isaac artist, wit, bullshitter and raconteur, although not necessarily in that order of importance. For that matter, Ted was also not necessarily celebrated. He painted the pebbles white and went on to decorate them with his original sketches and designs. There were no better souvenirs of Port Isaac to be obtained anywhere. Ted pitted his own artistry against that of the sea, and the result was a creditable no contest.

———

Just outside the little gug with its store of pebbles, a strange concretionary deposit composed of fragments of old iron was seemingly fused into the surrounding rocks. The boys assumed that the deposit represented a long-term accumulation of certain pieces of metallic debris heaved over Hillson's Dump, all assembled together in one place by crafty tidal currents. The deposit of old iron looked neat. Talk about a treat!

———

When the ebb tide fell to its lowest level, so many rocks broke the surface of the sea in the awn that the boys almost believed that they could jump from one rock to the other to ultimately stand on top of the Kenewal. "Almost" was the key qualification governing their subsequent inaction. Every rock bristled with gardens of kelp. The kelp fronds flopped down impotently around their stalks, denied the support and sustenance of the sea until the tide rose around them again.

The absence of a sub-tidal environment, however, was no more than a fleeting moment in the life of the kelp gardens. Very soon the tide would rise, bearing the kelp fronds up with it. The Kenewal would submerge like a U-boat. The kelp gardens would bloom on and around the Kenewal as always, waving in their secret depths.

Upper Fore Street, Port Isaac, with Canadian Terrace on the left

8

Turn-ups, Cab-bidge!

ALTHOUGH THE WAR WAS OVER, the burden of digging for victory as a patriotic duty was not easily shaken from the bent shoulders of even the more unwilling of those who, for the duration, made up Port Isaac's venerated host of garden and allotment tillers.

Old habits died hard. Home grown vegetables continued to be a common currency, nurtured under the rich caress of storm-wracked seaweed and of shit. The latter was either unadulterated or mixed with straw and derived from a variety of farmyard animals, dogs not included.

In their prime the gardens and allotments of Port Isaac were ranked up by their creators in the manner of armies ready for battle. There were razor-ridged rows of potatoes, files of onions standing at attention, clumped platoons of cabbages and cauliflowers, and vertiginous rows of runner beans commanding the high ground. Sometimes, a sentinel withy stood in a corner to inspect the parade.

The virtue of purposeful digging was evident in every handful of earth in which a vegetable found purchase. From the earth, the stony content was exiled as efficiently as were fleas from a boy's hair under the tearful sweep of a fine-toothed comb.

There was, as was known, no shortage of those for whom work as a concept, in or out of a garden, was something they would rather not be associated with, irrespective of digging for victory. After all, Fred Ball had it on good authority that when Harry Bluff went to hospital one day it was for an X-ray "to see if there do be any work in the bugger".

Whatever the event, as much for the benefit of the gardeners and allotment tillers who put their best foot forward onto the blade of a shovel as for the less industrious members of Port Isaac society, there would always be the Blake brothers' Saturday morning round to fall back on when cadging garden produce or surreptitiously lifting an occasional root under cover of darkness was a faded option.

———

The Blake brothers were two in number. They were incidentally identical twins. They were farmers. Their farm was named "Trewetha", naturally enough since the farmhouse was situated on the edge of the first corner where Trewetha Lane on its way out of Port Isaac towards Poltreworgey Hill made an "S" bend to negotiate its way through the sparsely populated hamlet of Trewetha.

Trewetha farmhouse had a well-kept, neat and clean appearance, which was not a feature that characterised too many of the other farms scattered around the parish. Certain of the other properties tended to resemble entrants in a competition to develop the most fetid morass covering their respective farmyards, into which items of rusting machinery, unwanted farmyard implements, and other objects best not thought about could be induced to sink without trace.

The Blake brothers were bustling, industrious men and, as far as the Port Isaac boys were concerned, they bore the great grace of treating the boys with kindly equanimity. The Blake brothers were not averse to the boys crossing their meadows with propriety, although the separate parties were never likely to define propriety in quite the same way.

The general attitude of most other farmers towards the boys was one of irate bellicosity. It seemed to take very little to generate such an attitude in a farmer's breast. On the other hand this was not always to the dismay of the boys, as it added spice to the enduring game of trespassing.

―――

The Blake brothers were named Sam and Will. When Sam appeared without Will, or when Will appeared without Sam, anyone they met up with was usually forced to guess, not always correctly, whether or not the Blake twin in view should be addressed as Sam or as Will. The boys countered the dilemma by addressing both of them as Mr Blake.

When Sam and Will were seen out together, then maybe there were subtle differences in their joint aspect which could be detected with care by experts, but even so, saying for sure which one was Sam and which one was Will was never going to be easy. Sam and Will were equally lean and stringy in form. They strode along, angling forward, lantern jaws leading the way. Each of them affected a steady grin that seemed wholly genuine and at ease, once a close scrutiny had managed to weed out its few vacant elements.

―――

Sam and Will dressed alike, for convenience rather than style. On their feet they wore sea boots of vintage rubber, on which a sizeable proportion of farm soil was coated for safekeeping. Their trousers were of coarse cloth, bearing both natural and not so natural stains, and were held up with braces of a perished elasticity that would have been truly exciting in the context of knickers. The drooping quality of the braces was given sustenance, sometimes, with a length of hairy binder twine wound around the trouser waist.

The Blake brothers' jackets, which had competed with all aspects of prevalent weather and had not only lost that struggle but had failed as well in any endeavour to match up with the trousers, were ripped for proper effect in at least two places. The pockets of the jackets sagged not only under the weight of a long-term accumulation of a range of forgotten items, some of which may have once been useful, but also in memory of the fact that at one time the jackets had had pretensions to being new, but that time was not now.

Sam and Will's shirts were collarless, although a collar stud was invariably in place just in case the need for formality should rear its unwelcome head. Over the shirt and under the jacket they sported waistcoats buttoned up with as many buttons as had not yet dropped off, waistcoats unrelated to trousers and jacket to the regret of neither.

———

On their heads Sam and Will wore flat caps, the exteriors of which bore clear witness to the fact that the interiors contained sweatbands.

Flat caps were as individual as personal fingerprints in the manner in which they were worn. A trusty cap of many years' standing moulded itself to the head beneath as perfectly as did any remaining hair. Sam and Will wore their flat caps as square on the head, with identical clearance over each ear, as if the caps had been set in place using a spirit level.

———

Every Saturday morning during the appropriate farming season when all was being gathered in 'ere the winter storms begin, Sam and Will, with the erratic assistance of Mr Bill Masters, made a tour around the streets of Port Isaac leading a horse-drawn cart. The cart was mounded improbably high with a cargo of firm-hearted round cabbages and big turnips pulled so recently from the fields that great gobs of soil still clung to them.

Only the best of the Blake brothers' turnips, golden bottomed and purple topped under a crown of breeze-bobbled fresh green leaves were pulled for sale to the Port Isaac public. Their lesser cousins were left in the ground for sheep to chomp down to recessed rotting hollows in which the cold winter rain pooled.

Some boys took occasional turnips from Sam and Will's fields as well, when they were out on their wanderings. They lifted one turnip each, stripped away the leaves, wiped off as much of the coating soil as they could on the nearest patch of grass, held the turnip by the stalk, tore off the skin with their teeth, and gnawed the juicy flesh with the utmost satisfaction as they proceeded.

Sam and Will's horse was a big brown carthorse whose massively shod hooves clopped and chunked ponderously on the hard road. The horse must have enjoyed being placed between the hafts of a two-wheeled wooden cart for a leisurely walk around the village. It made a welcome break from his other duties of dragging one or another implement of heavy farm machinery across soggy fields.

The cartwheels were fine examples of the wheelwright's art. They were taller than most of the boys, wooden-spoked and bound with steel around their circumferences. They crunched and rumbled over the many trembling irregularities in the road surface as Sam and Will's round made its regular way.

Old Bill Masters always followed behind the cart. Bill wore his flat cap at a rather jaunty angle, slouched over one of his ears.

Bill, known as "Bill Bumps", was a cheerful type, short and rotund. He had a rather quizzical look on his face as if he was never quite sure of either where he was or what he was doing there in the first place. It was said that Bill Bumps was a victim of shelling in the Great War, and he was reputed to have a metal plate set in the top of his head.

The metal plate was supposed to be visible when Bill Bumps took his cap off, but since he never appeared without that selfsame half-cocked item firmly in place, the secret of the metal plate was to that extent secure. All attempts by the boys to get Bill Bumps to take his cap off never met with any success.

As Bill Bumps and Sam (or Will) Blake plodded behind and alongside the mighty load of turnips and cabbages through the streets of Port Isaac, Bill Bumps kept up a constant chant of "TUR-nups CAB-bidge! TUR-nups CAB-bidge!", in tones which were as penetrating as they were strident, a clarion call to customers to come out and make their purchases.

The passage of the cart was marked by a dribbling trail of soil, punctuated here and there by a steamy mound of horseshit. The soil remained on the road for the rain to wash away but the horseshit was a prize too good to be ignored and was gathered up and whipped away in a bucket by the lucky gardener who arrived first on the scene, well before even a single fly had had a chance to investigate its surface.

The "TUR-nups CAB-bidge!" cry was infectious. Boys joined in the cavalcade, bawling the slogan in concert with Bill Bumps.

—

Bill Bumps darted at the boys, flailing his hands to chase them away. He was at great pains, however, not to catch any of them and thereby place the security of his cap at risk from fingers ready to flip it up and off in an instant.

View of Khandalla and the allotments looking across the school playground
and the harbour from the front of number 7, Canadian Terrace

Downtown Port Isaac. Margaret's Lane rises through sunshine on the upper left

9

At the Top of Margaret's Lane

NOT MORE THAN FIFTY YARDS up along Trewetha Lane above Doctor's Surgery, set slightly back on the right hand side behind a very small and less than even surfaced open area, were located the garage cum coal storage building facilities of Mr J. H. Spry, the Port Isaac coalman.

The building was walled and roofed over in corrugated sheet metal. Its roof was appropriately decorated with a thick deposit of tar. Within the building was to be found Mr J. H. Spry's stock of coal and a ramshackle flat-backed lorry with which to deliver the same to his customers.

In the noble tradition of the Port Isaac county primary school headmaster, Mr C. Victor Richards, the only one of Mr J. H. Spry's godfather-given initials that counted for anything much was the second one. In the case of Mr J. H. Spry, the H stood for Harold.

Contrary to the institutionalised nature of Port Isaac nick-naming practice, however, in the case of Mr J. H. Spry, Harold was not reduced to Harry, as it was with Mr Harry Hills the village undertaker or with Mr Harry May, otherwise known as Harry Bluff, who to certain knowledge had never been known to undertake anything much. Nor was Harold shortened to the ulti-mate 'Arr as it had been with the curmudgeonly Mr 'Arr Oaten who lived over in Rose Hill.

Some of those fortunate or unfortunate enough, depending

on the point of view, to be given the name of Harold were born for relegation to mere Harry, and some others – well one anyway, so it seemed – to subside even further down the scale. Yet where Mr J. H. Spry was concerned he was christened Harold, Harold fit him like a glove, and so Harold he was destined to be in perpetuity.

———

Harold Spry was slight in figure. He was mild mannered and temperate of habits and disposition. Harold was undoubtedly one of nature's supreme and genuine gentlemen. It was only necessary to look at the way Harold conducted himself to appreciate at once that he was a chapel man from head to toe. Harold looked like a man who in all probability would have been at home in the presence of any of the rousing hymns of Mr Sankey.

Harold was indeed a chorister of note. For an enduring time he was one of the four members of a vocal group, not unsurprisingly a quartet, which called itself the "Four in Harmony". The Four in Harmony also featured Mr John Prout, the elder of the celebrated Prout Bros of public bus transport fame, and Mr Jack Collings, a gentleman blessed with a scintillating array of daughters that gave him about the same amount of bother that he gave them.

The Four in Harmony came together to sing regularly at concerts in either the Temperance Hall or the Church Rooms. They inevitably performed at many chapel functions, although they didn't discriminate at all in terms of creed. Increasing age may have induced their glory days to be then rather than now, but they were rarely backwards to come forward to provide a captive audience with a number or two from their reasonably melodious repertoire.

Typically, the Four in Harmony might open a performance with a rendition of "Silver Threads Among the Gold". That always went down very well with an audience, and the first line, "Darling, I am growing older", could have served to define any one of the Four. They were known to be great admirers of the famous American close harmony ensemble, "The Inkspots", and were ever-inclined to follow up "Silver Threads" with a popular Inkspots number, of which "Bless You, For Being an Angel" was a perennial favourite.

———

Harold's intimate association with the delivery of Port Isaac's vital supply of domestic coal, or alternatively coke (or even anthracite once in a while), was thought by certain of the Port Isaac boys to establish him as a kind of "Old King Coal". They couldn't help but think of the traditional rhyme and accompanying tune when they saw Harold out making his coal delivery round. To cap it all, in the company of the Four in Harmony, Harold was well in the presence of a tailor made "fiddlers three".

———

For all that he was spare of frame, Harold was equipped with a broad back and powerful arms. His physique was developed by the accustomed hauling of hundredweight bags of coal, referred to by his customers as "hunderds", to domestic destinations well beyond those where his lorry could be induced to gain proximity. In this pursuit, Harold toiled up and down flights of steps of assorted lengths and steepness of inclination, and in and out of alleys, opes and lanes characterised as often as not by the fact that their dimensions could have been a lot more accommodating than they were to a man bearing a hunderd of coal on his back.

Harold heaved and dumped coal into a range of sheds, dark cellars, rat-ridden bunkers and, so it was reliably rumoured, certain baths of the portable zinc and fixed enamelled white varieties. Everyone knew that there were residents of Baul council houses who stored coal in their baths, although given their location on the near side of Wadebridge, the Baul council houses were a bit too far away from Port Isaac for Harold to deliver the essential coal to them for such storage.

In the full practice of his profession Harold clad himself in a leather apron and leather hooded shoulder cape, both of which were invested with the true colour and accumulated memory of many more tons derived from carried hunderds of coal than could reasonably be counted.

The upper side of Harold's garage and coal yard was bounded by a narrow lane, known officially as "Margaret's Lane", the descending course of which linked Trewetha Lane to the lower part of Rose Hill. Margaret's Lane made, as a matter of choice, a convenient short cut to downtown Port Isaac.

Margaret's Lane sank resignedly towards Rose Hill in the manner of a dark stone dropped into a tub of black treacle. It was narrower, deeper and much steeper by far than Church Hill ever could be. Blackthorn bushes fingered in from either side and clutched at each other overhead, providing the upper part of Margaret's Lane with the look of a tunnel leading down into the pit of doom. It was not an inappropriate adjunct to Harold's coal yard.

The children of Port Isaac knew Margaret's Lane by the more familiar title of "Witchy Andrews' Lane", commemorating a lady named Miss (or Mrs Andrews, none of them knew for sure) who lived in a gloomy cottage about half way down the lane between Trewetha Lane and Rose Hill. It was a lot easier for Harold to carry Witchy Andrews' coal down from above than to haul it up from below.

Witchy Andrews was gravely wizened by the shadow of her advancing years. She shared her cottage with a small flock of cats, which sinister association, coupled with her extremely whiskery features, talon-like hands, lank and dirty grey hair that regarded soap as a stranger, and manner of ragged attire that even a church jumble sale stall would have had difficulties in stocking let alone selling, did little to unsettle her reputation as a likely member of a coven in the eyes of the children.

Witchy Andrews' cottage was on the left hand side, the first cottage to be passed on the way down. Its door was always open. Scraggy, yellow-eyed constituents of her feline familiars could be observed moving about in the grainy darkness within. The smell of cats and of fish that was no longer fresh was a tangible presence around the cottage. The only missing feature in this sombre prospect was that of a broomstick, leaning against the peeling doorframe, ready and waiting.

Passing by the cottage, especially if it was known that Witchy Andrews was at home, was done by children only as a dare. It required courage to undertake. Those who dared crept down slowly; ready to flee back up again if they met Witchy Andrews coming towards them. Once near her cottage door they took to their heels and ran on past as hard as they could, not stopping until they reached the sanctuary of Rose Hill.

———

As it was, Witchy Andrews rarely ventured down the Lane named after her. She almost invariably took the ascent, and then turned right at the top to ply her way along Trewetha Lane as far as the group of fish merchants' (otherwise known as "fish jouders") cellars just above where Rose Hill and Trewetha Lane came together at the pointy corner called "First and Last".

Witchy Andrews' target at the fish jouders' cellars was the bins in which the fish jouders disposed of backbones and offal from the fish that they gutted, cleaned and filleted on the premises. Her bent figure was a not unfamiliar sight, doubled over the bins and clawing through the contained mess of bones and guts. Every now and then she lifted up a long dripping spine and inspected it as if she was about to dedicate it to dark forces.

Witchy Andrews spoke to few, and of those few, fewer still responded. Her tattered grimness and gaunt eyes inspired a shiver of fear in too many of those who encountered her. She walked with hunched shoulders over folded arms in a kind of forward thrusting motion that was eerie and aggressive at the same time.

Witchy Andrews returned to her cottage from the fish jouders' cellars by the way she had come. She turned left by Harold's coal yard, laden with fishy booty. The boys dared not think what she planned to do with it. However, no doubt her flock of cats would have been happy enough to offer them an opinion.

——

On the other corner made by Witchy Andrews' Lane with Trewetha Lane, opposite to the one at the side of Harold's coal yard, was a small stone-walled and slate-roofed barn belonging to Mr Tom Saundry.

Tom lived downtown alongside the flowing Lake in the heart of Middle Street with his two unmarried sisters, Etta and Beattie, and his much younger brother Joe. There they kept a rudimentary shop, stocking vegetables grown by Tom and sour-looking apples picked from dank and ivy-hung trees, all begging to be pruned, in a barbed wire protected orchard that Tom owned way up in the Port Isaac valley.

Etta and Beattie ran the shop. They were a kindly pair. Tom's function in the enterprise was to upset customers and passers by alike with a power of personality that had turned grousing and taciturnity into a consistent art form.

Tom favoured the wearing of insistently muddy hobnailed boots. He scraped the hobnails on the ground in a shambling walk with one shoulder held high and his neck thrust forward, his head bobbing impatiently at the end of it.

——

The interior of Tom's little barn at the top of Witchy Andrews' Lane was a monument to a wardrobe philosophy of never throwing anything away since you never knew when it might come in handy. The arrangement and storage of the over-prolific junk in the barn was so meticulously neat and tidy as to have been clearly made with the most loving of care spread over sufficient generations to ensure that whatever lay at the back was a mystery.

The door on the upper side of the barn could at least be

opened, but inside the door the barn was crammed so full of bits and pieces, abundant odds and ends and a horn of plenty of general scrap, that getting in, even to shelter from the rain under the wormy lintel, was just about out of the question.

———

Harold's garage was not as packed out as Tom's barn, but it was full enough when the coal supplies came in. His sluggish delivery lorry might then have to be parked in the yard area for a while. On the right hand side of the sliding door to the garage, a tap with an attached length of rubber hose provided water with which Harold washed down the lorry from time to time.

Some of the less charitable of his Port Isaac customers, who were a lot easier to identify than the more charitable, claimed that Harold's lorry washing practice also took in the sacks of coal, by which means Harold was able to temporarily improve the cohesiveness of the coal slack that his customers abhorred so much. Neither was the addition of water entirely detrimental to bolstering the weight of coal in a sack.

———

Harold's lorry was a comfortingly familiar sight as it crept and crawled on its rounds of Port Isaac. It moved with such supreme economy of speed that Ted Robinson declared its make to be a "Rolls Canardly"."It rolls downhill all right", said Ted, "but it can 'ardly get back up again!"

It was once alleged that a pedestrian had passed Harold's lorry, although to give him the benefit of the doubt, the pedestrian might have been taking a brisk walk at the time. Then again, it being Port Isaac, walking briskly was not really all that likely.

When Harold's lorry was out and about it became a magnet for boys intent on obtaining what they called a "tow". Towing was a ritual practice involving hanging on to the back of the lorry and trotting (or walking, never running) behind it as it proceeded along its way.

———

When the lorry load of hunderds of coal was high enough, Harold was seemingly oblivious to the presence of the boys on tow at the time. The best kind of tow was in the province of those with hobnails on their boots since hobnails allowed them to slide along the road as if they were skating on ice.

If there were not enough individual handholds for all Harold's clandestine passengers desirous of a tow, then the boys linked hands to hold onto one another. It was common enough for a chain of as many as twenty boys to be linked up on tow behind Harold's lorry as it weaved its leisurely way about its business.

When Harold stopped the lorry to get out and unload a hunderd or two, the boys on tow let go of the lorry and stood innocently around until Harold got back in, started up, and the lorry moved off again.

———

Harold did not approve of towing boys, but as a one-man operation he was powerless to do much about it. Harold's periodic admonishments of the boys were possibly the only occasions on which his gentlemanly principles slipped sufficiently to permit a measure of imprudent language to intrude.

Generally, an unspoken truce existed between Harold and the boys he towed, brought about by resignation to the inevitable on Harold's part, and by the usual dogged persistence on theirs.

*Lower Dolphin Street joining up with Middle Street
at the bottom*

St Peter's church, Port Isaac

10

In Church

THE FRONT WALL OF ST PETER'S CHURCH faced towards Back Hill, suggesting that the architect of the barn-like edifice was blessed with a sense of humour that was found to be all too frequently lacking in the more regular members of the church congregation. The same front wall was pierced by a set of three tall, narrow-pointed windows, fitted out with an ornate array of tiny panes of clear glass held together by strips of lead. Twin buttresses supported the front wall on the outside of the church in a gesture not unrelated to the presence of an old mineshaft sunk into the adjoining bank that sloped down to Back Hill below. The two buttresses stood on either side of the group of windows, and a wooden bench fitted between them provided a pleasant enough spot for sitting on a sunny day.

The entire complement of stained glass windows at St Peter's was located at the back end of the church. The back end, of course, was the end that faced towards Front Hill. The stained glass windows formed a dominant backdrop to the altar and offered a cheerful illumination to the choir stalls through their bright and vivid panes. They were such an essential part of the spirit of the church that they were taken for granted.

A combined grouping of three stained glass windows, matching the window configuration at the front of the church, soared like skyrockets from directly behind the altar. Two more of such, one of which was added sometime after the war in memory of a celebrated long serving former vicar, the Rev. Martin, graced the church wall on the left of the altar behind the double bank of choir stalls.

The trio of stained glass windows behind the altar was partially obscured from the view of anyone sitting in the nave of the church by a redundant censer hanging in the field of view over the central gap in the altar rail.

The centre window of the three depicted a classic portrayal of Jesus on the cross. Details of the scene, all picked out in telling colour, consisted of sword-induced wounds, the heads of nails penetrating flesh, running blood, a halo and three seemingly impotent angels hovering overhead, all united in their failure to have averted the carnage. No young mind could fail to be impressed.

On the window to the left of this gory feature, in a further tribute to the stained glass maker's art, a complicated nativity scene was offered. Its counterpoint window, over on the right, provided what was if anything an even more intricate composition related to the Presentation of the child Jesus in the Temple.

The stained glass window on the side immediately to the left of the altar behind the choir stalls was much simpler in concept. It contained a full-length view of an elderly St Peter clad in full bishop's regalia. The keys to the kingdom were hanging from his left hand. One key appeared to have been cast in silver and one in gold. It was St Peter's church after all, and its patron saint had every right to be on view.

The stained glass window commemorating the Rev. Martin's contribution to St Peter's church carried another full-length portrait, this one of a youngish St Paul, younger than St Peter that is, although looking rather more hirsute than the latter. According to Miss Jessie Pidler, St Paul was the Rev. Martin's "favourite saint". Jessie, whose consistent diligence in attending church services provided an example that few were able to emulate, or really wished to be able to emulate, clearly missed those good old days when the Rev. Martin held forth from the pulpit.

However, the Rev. Martin had had his day, and now was now, and the vicar on the spot after the war was the Rev. W. Atterbury Thomas. Apart from being yet another prominent resident of Port Isaac who chose to initialise his first Christian name (or maybe his only Christian name as it could be open to debate whether or not Atterbury qualified for that distinction), the Rev. W. Atterbury Thomas was meet and right to be numbered among the very best of men.

Moreover, the Rev. W. Atterbury Thomas was the very model of a modern rural vicar. He was urbane, compassionate, and wore his faith like a badge. His jug ears and bald head were the icing on the cake. The Rev. W. Atterbury Thomas believed totally in his vocation. If ever there was glory to be found in the tangled bosom of the church, then the glory resided in such men as the Rev. W. Atterbury Thomas, of whom hymns should be sung in praise.

St Peter's church, safe under the imperial aegis of the Rev. W. Atterbury Thomas, provided a true point of focus not only for the individual and united lives of its congregation but also for many others who were somewhat more reluctant to identify themselves too openly with a religious routine. A social routine was quite another matter, however, and if it was necessary to make a show of falling in line with the religious part in order to qualify for the outings and parties, well, Amen to that.

The rite of the St Peter's church congregational year was ticked off by successive Sunday services, attendance at Sunday school and the regularity of church social events inclusive of meetings of the Mothers' Union, the St Peter's PT Club, and youth fellowship. The great annual bonuses were in the Christmas party, the August fête in the grounds of the Church Rooms, the jumble sale, the summer outing to the seaside (as if Port Isaac people didn't see enough of the seaside already) and a January visit to the pantomime at the Palace Theatre in Plymouth.

Although there were occasions when it might be deemed necessary for boys whose families were church-oriented to attend a service at St Peter's church during the week, thank goodness such an imposition did not come along very often. Sad to say, however, Good Friday was a notorious exception, as on that day the vicar held a bleak, three-hour long service in a church that was devoid of colour, apart that is from a gloomy purple altar cloth.

The format of the Good Friday service consisted of a droning, mind numbing sequence of fifteen-minute sermons that were prevented from colliding with one another only by the punctuation of a selection of the more dreary *A&M* hymns. Prior to Good Friday the vicar informed the Sunday school and choir boys, in no uncertain terms, that since Jesus was about to give up his life for them, the least they could do in return was give up an hour or so to him on his big day.

The boys were permitted to exit the church at the Good Friday service only during the hymn singing intervals, but they were trapped in their seats when the sermons were crawling along their morose path. No choir sat in the stalls on Good Friday – something of a blessing for those of the boys who were choir members – however, choir boys in particular were ordered by the vicar to be present in the nave of the church for the duration of at least three sermons and linking hymns, and the boys knew that the vicar kept tally on their attendance from the pulpit.

James was a member of the choir, hence a choirboy. He couldn't sing, but in the St Peter's church choir that failing didn't make him in any way unique. His sense of duty was unable to survive through any more than one Good Friday sermon segment, after which his powers of enduring further torment gave up the ghost as surely as Jesus was reported to have done on the first Good Friday. Fifteen minutes of listening to what William Shakespeare described as "the parson's saw" felt to James more like fifteen hours.

One year James used the excuse of feeling ill, which was really not too wide of the mark, to escape from church after just one sermon on Good Friday. Unfortunately, that was not a ruse that could be used twice, as too many other boys came to discover as well. Live now and pay later was then their preferred option. The vicar's inevitable wrath to be called down on them next week after the passage of Easter was but a small price for the boys to pay for an early escape to the open air on Good Friday.

——

The church vestry, where the choirboys met before services, was adjoined to the back of the church on the right side of the sanctuary. The vestry contained two rooms. The outer room, directly inside the vestry entry door at the foot of the sloping path coming down towards the church from Front Hill, was the larger of the two. The bell rope hung on one side just inside the door. A curtain screening the vestry off from the church was just across on the right of anyone who entered, close enough to be touched by a long arm.

In the outer room of the vestry the church organist, those members of the church choir who had bothered or, alternatively, had been forced to turn up, and the vicar's curate when there was one, all assembled prior to services to don their individual red cassocks, their much hated frilly ruffs and their barely tolerated white surplices.

Although a useful debate might have been held at any time to determine how appropriate the title of "choir" might have been when applied to the few who made up its company, and the even fewer among them who could carry an adequate tune, it never happened. The choir had a certain cosmetic appeal when set up in a stall in numbers present greater than one, and that was justification enough for its existence.

The attitude of the choirboys to the vestry was shaped by an old joke that did the rounds so often that it became identified in their minds with St Peter's church: "Next Tuesday being Ash

Wednesday," the story ran, "there will be an open-air meeting of the church committee in the vestry. Admission will be free. Please pay at the door. Take a seat and sit on the floor. The meeting will be presided over by a gentleman-lady sitting at a corner of the round table, and the committee will decide which colour the church shall be whitewashed."

———

The outer room of the vestry was a reasonably cheerful place. Even the short-term presence in the choir of a school bully who was a particular expert in knuckling the ribs of small boys did not dampen choral spirits for long. Small boys were accustomed to that kind of treatment at school and had learned to live with it. The intervals before and after church services, especially on those increasingly rare occasions when there were a fair number of choir members in attendance, gave the vestry the atmosphere of a warm-hearted boys club.

As such great times the choirboys generally managed to subdue their customary hubbub before services commenced but considered themselves tied by no constraints when services were over. The irate ministrations of the churchwardens came to be regularly visited upon them to quell the clamour from the vestry that threatened to drown out the organist's closing voluntaries.

———

The inner vestry room was much smaller than the outer, to which it was annexed. The inner room was the sole preserve of the vicar. The vicar's array of vestments, which varied in colour and adornment in blind accordance with the specifications of the church calendar, were stored away in a trunk, together with matching altar cloths, pulpit drapes, altar candles and other key regalia.

A chalice and paten, brought out into the light on the first Sunday of each month for the purposes of serving wine and wafers to respectively represent the blood and body of Christ to the confirmed at Holy Communion services, were kept under lock and key in the inner room. Both items gleamed bright and golden as they emerged from captivity. As to whether or not the chalice and paten were genuinely made of gold, it was nice to think that they were, even though they probably weren't.

———

The stock of wine was confined under an even more secure lock than was the chalice. Delivered directly from the vicar's hands at a scheduled juncture in the Holy Communion service, the ration of wine swigged by communicants was, certainly in James's confirmed experience, barely enough to even moisten the tongue. For his personal taste the communion wine was much too sweet. He regarded the drop of moisture that the wine provided as absolutely essential to help him shift the communion wafer from the roof of his mouth, where it always seemed to fuse like a second skin, defying all his efforts to lick it off.

After communion service, the wine remaining in the chalice, of which there always seemed to be more than a little, (some suspected by design), was knocked back by the vicar in the privacy of his inner room in the vestry. He crossed himself at first to add legitimacy to the pending enjoyment. He then poured a small measure of water, presumably of the holy variety, into the chalice from a small bottle. Any wafer crumbs left on the paten were swept into the chalice as well. The vicar swirled the holy brew around for a bit, and, crossing himself for a second time, swilled it down in a trice.

The empty chalice was wiped dry and was locked away, pending its next outing. If the chalice was ever washed in a sink with soap, only the vicar knew for sure. In any case, regular communicants swore that the holiness of the chalice ensured that any germs coming into contact with its rim would be instantly destroyed.

———

It was also to the inner room in the vestry that the churchwardens, Messrs John Neal and Westlake Brown, came after services to count and verify the amount of collection made during the service. John was the "vicar's warden", and Westlake (or "Wesslick") was the "people's warden". The collection was characterised by the preponderance of pennies that it contained. No doubt John and Wesslick counted themselves lucky if there were fewer halfpennies in the take.

The way the collection was made was that the churchwardens each worked their own particular side of the church. Viewed from the altar, looking towards the nave, John's seat, equipped with its staff of office, stood on the aisle in the back row on the left. Wesslick's equivalent was a row or two forward across the aisle on the right.

John and Wesslick moved from the back to the front of the nave, row by row, each handing a little red embroidered felt collection bag along one line and receiving the bag again when it was returned along the line ahead.

Donations to collections were made anonymously in all cases save one. The contributed coinage (a ten bob note would have represented a true miracle) was released from the hands of the donors inside the collection bag. As long as the donors could arrange to generate the chink of one coin impacting on another, whether or not they had genuinely put in anything in the first place, the collection bag's honour was satisfied.

One boy claimed that he dropped a penny in a bag and took out a sixpenny piece. It was a feat so admired in the telling that some others tried to repeat it, although without the same degree of success.

The cited lack of anonymity occurred in the choir stalls, where a third collection bag, exclusive to the members of the choir, was passed. If only one member of the choir was present, not an uncommon event, the contents of the choir stalls' collection bag would have to be deemed to have come from that very person. In James's case the contribution would amount to the sum of one copper penny that his mother gave him for the purpose. Even so, that was a penny more than St Peter's sometimes got from him when the ranks of the choir were greater and retaining the penny for his personal use was a preferred option.

———

Having relieved the congregation of its cumulative collection proceeds, John and Wesslick advanced up the steps from the nave to the sanctuary, and strode heavily towards the altar between the facing choir stalls. The pair of them were made ponderous by a sense of occasion and self importance rather than by the weight of whatever was in the collection bags. One or the other of the duo performed a little foot shuffle at the head of the nave to ensure they were in step.

Once counted and recorded, the collection takings were salted away with absolute prudence by John, who held the post of church treasurer in addition to that of being the vicar's churchwarden.

At Easter, all the proceeds of the collections went into the vicar's pocket. This was one of the rights of his living. For some weeks prior to the arrival of Easter the vicar took every possible opportunity to remind the congregation of his coming benefit, and if he didn't exactly issue the edict to "Give generously", he implied it in a hundred and one ways through his educated mastery of language.

The vicar's faith in the generosity of the congregation was matched by his hope that substantive charity would be forthcoming from the latter. The latter's response was in tune with sounding brass or a tinkling cymbal.

———

Two regular church services took place on Sundays. Choirboys like James were required to attend at least one of them. It was when they were promoted to serve at the altar that they were unable to make a choice as to which service they attended.

Matins (and sermon) commenced at eleven o'clock in the morning, apart from the first Sunday in the month when Holy

Communion (regrettably also with sermon) replaced it. Evensong (and the inevitable sermon) came along at six o'clock, not unnaturally, in the evening. Sunday school, for which attendance was quite mandatory, fell in between the two stools, starting at two o'clock. All of the services, not excepting Sunday school, seemed timed to be endured for about an hour.

The choirboys who attended Matins barely had time to change out of their cassocks and chew through their Sunday roast dinner before the time to return to the church for Sunday school rolled along. So it became a better regarded option for them to engage in Sunday school and Evensong. This left the morning free, there was less need to rush through dinner unless the meat was tougher than usual, and there were still a few hours available on Sunday afternoon to go out along the cliffs.

———

The popularity of combining Sunday school with Evensong had the consequence of seriously depleting the numbers present in the choir stalls at Matins. As a consequence, in order to ensure the presence of at least one choirboy at Matins, to serve at altar if nothing else, the vicar introduced a rota. None of the choirboys liked it, but there it was, the vicar was the law.

One benefit of Evensong for the seasoned drinkers of the congregation (do not call them legion for they were not many), who found comfort in believing that time spent sitting in the church neutralised any criticism of the much greater time they spent in the public bar of the Golden Lion, was that the service closed at precisely the time when the Golden Lion opened its doors to its own faithful. Evensong, unlike Matins, did not cut into productive drinking time.

———

James was one who eventually drew regular duty to serve at the altar, and made a lonely figure in the choir stalls as often as not. The server's job incorporated three key elements. The first of these was to light, and later on at the correct time in the order of the service, to extinguish the huge candles mounted one on each side of the altar. The candles were lit shortly before the service commenced and snuffed out during the hymn sung prior to the sermon.

The implement used for lighting the candles was a long wooden staff fitted with a taper holder attached to a conical candlesnuffer, both wrought in brass, on one end. James undertook the ritual with all due solemnity, criss-crossing in front of the altar, first to light the left hand candle and then to light the right hand one from a waxed taper slotted into the holder. The waxed taper was lit beforehand with a match in the vestry. As James passed before the ornate brass cross at the centre of the altar, he faced it, stopped briefly, and bowed his head before moving on.

Extinguishing the candles required the exact same order of ritual as did their lighting, this time employing the conical snuffer, lowered over the candle flame. The art of this exercise lay in the control with which it was performed. James learned through experience that when he lowered the snuffer slowly and gently onto the candle flame causing the flame to expire, the wick of the candle was induced to hold on to a valiant spark that smouldered away happily for the balance of the service.

The steady spark generated wispy sinews of candle smoke. These sifted their way from the altar down through the sanctuary and into the church nave, where they wove like wraiths through the congregation present. Sometimes, when James was very exact with his snuffing technique, the pungent odour of smouldering candles might make it all the way back to where Wesslick and John were sitting in their staff-girt chairs.

—

The second task for a server was to lead the procession of the members of the choir into the sanctuary from the vestry at the commencement of the service, and back out again when the service was, fortunately, all over.

Leading a procession in and out of course had to assume that there was a procession to be led in the first place. As a server, James found himself not infrequently leading in a procession of one, namely himself.

———

Carving his name into the wood of the choir stall with a penknife eased James's solitary vigil through the dirge of many sermons, but finally his name came to be incised deeply enough for perpetuity's sake, and he had then to adapt his mind to other things, of which listening to a sermon was not ever going to be one if he could help it.

James was frequently reduced to reading hymns in *Hymns A&M* during sermons, as a result of which he learned large numbers of hymns by heart. He occasionally studied the baffling means of calculating the date of Easter using the tables provided in the Book of Common Prayer. Now and then he kept a weather eye on the ever-dwindling congregation down below.

———

One Sunday at Evensong, once again as the sole occupant of the choir stalls, James, as he had so often done before, pulled his surplice down and stretched it tightly over his cassocked knees during a sermon. The surplice may well have been washed once too often, as it parted from top to bottom with a resounding rip that echoed through the church, and seemed to rattle the stained glass windows as it did so. The vicar's hectoring harangue to the congregation hesitated for a breathless instant before resuming.

Any noise emanating from the choir stalls was a sure way to get the vicar to punctuate a sermon. His attention was generally directed at gossiping between choirboys when more than one of them was present, and was invariably accompanied by a well-rehearsed venomous look in their direction. The intent behind such looks must have broken at least one of the Ten Commandments, and maybe more than one.

Heads jerked among the congregation as the coursing rip of James's surplice cut through to them. Faces took on the aspect of

"It wasn't me!" nonchalance layered over acute embarrassment that was certain to appear in any genteel company when someone who was present broke wind.

———

The perpetrator in instances of surreptitious farting was usually the one among the gathering who looked the most innocent. It applied particularly to those who were able to release that prince of farts, that is to say the silent one, which not only filled the most space, but which was also by far the ripest of the bunch.

A standard playground riddle was, "What travels faster, wind or sound?" The answer was, "Wind, because no sooner does a fart leave your ass than it's up your nose for shelter!"

Silent farts were blessed with the quality of being combustible. As an impressive party trick, they could be ignited with a match to produce a swift haze of blue flame. However, this was not a trick that anyone ever saw performed at the St Peter's Sunday school Christmas party, although the chapel Sunday school Christmas party could have been another matter.

———

The ripped cassock presented James with a monumental dilemma as to how he could manage to fulfil the third key task of being a server at the altar, which was to stand at the very gates of the altar facing the congregation head on during the singing of the final hymn of the order of service, in order to receive the proceeds of the collection from John and Wesslick.

James deferred the moment of truth for as long as he could while the collection bags were making their impecunious way from the back to the front of the nave. Then, clutching the shreds of his surplice together, James scuttled from the choir stalls to the altar, and with the best ceremonial genuflection that he could manage under the circumstances, grabbed the round brass tray on which the collection bags were to be deposited, and moved to stand at attention in the required location.

Regulations called for the brass tray to be held at the level, but under the circumstances James held it in a vertical position against his chest. The tray just about hid the torn surplice from the view of the congregation. As John and Wesslick drew very close, James flipped the brass tray to its horizontal position for the deposition of the collection bags, then turned at once on one heel and toe to face the altar and present the collection to the ever-eager hands of the vicar.

James spun around so rapidly that the collection bags slid sideways on the polished surface of the brass tray. It seemed that they might shoot off towards the Mother's Union banner over the left, but fate was kind in allowing him to arrest the slide with his right hand, just in time.

He regained the safety of the choir stalls shielded from the view of the congregation by the best Sunday suited backs of John and Wesslick as they plodded ahead of him, naturally in step, towards their waiting seats.

John and Wesslick, in performing their role as the two official pillars of St Peter's church, were provided with unofficial support by three equally pillar-like maiden ladies. The absence of any one of the three old ladies from any given church services implied a serious illness, a sudden death or perhaps the fact that she may have been lost in the lavatory.

Their respective names were the aforementioned Miss Jessie Pidler, who lived in a terraced house a good stiff walk up along Church Hill, Miss Alice Brown, who resided in a detached cottage on Rose Hill with her brother (none other than Wesslick), and a certain Miss Furze, whose bungalow was in the lower part of Trewetha Lane, a stone's throw from St Peter's church.

Alice was short, slightly stout, stern faced, and hawk like in her manner, all of which characteristics overlay the kindest of hearts.

Miss Furze had no Christian name that any the boys knew of. They called her "Fanny Fuzz Bush". Individual fuzz bushes made up the impenetrable jungles of furze, or gorse, that carpeted so many slopes out in the valleys. Fanny Fuzz Bush was an archetypal sweet old lady of rosy cheeks and dainty manner.

Jessie lived with her brother Frederick, who was even older than she was. When Frederick passed away, a wrought iron gate in his memory was erected across the top of the path leading up to St Peter's church from Back Hill. The gate was never locked shut, and it made not a bad facility for the boys to swing on, always in the name of Frederick.

The cross that Jessie had to bear was her surname. Any mention of it among the boys, as in "Here comes Miss Pidler", was certain to provoke either a good stifled giggle or a wave of guffaws, the volume of such depending on how far away Jessie was at the time. It was such an unfortunate name to have been burdened with that a convention was developed by which Jessie was normally referred to by all and sundry as "Miss Pedlar".

A plaque mounted on Frederick's memorial gate, however, referred to Mr Fredrick Pidler, and even went so far as to spell Frederick's surname correctly, much to the merriment of the Sunday school stalwarts who never missed a chance to read the inscription on the plaque out loud on the way in.

Jessie was quite frail, and as she plied the regular way between her home and St Peter's church, she never failed to look much better than one who was lightly spiced up for an impending encounter with the grim reaper. She always sat in the aisle seat of the very front left hand row of chairs in the nave, two rows in front of Alice. In that seat Jessie was closest to the pulpit, and from it she could have thrown, had she but had the strength and were she so inclined, a book of *Hymns A&M* to hit the entry to the vestry on the other side of the organ.

Notwithstanding the fact that their individual residences stood at widely disparate distances from the church door, Jessie, Alice and Fanny Fuzz Bush usually managed to make an acceptably synchronized arrival at the church door for services. They were drawn by the insistent clanging of the church bell, inserting their respective departures from home into appropriate junctures of its tolling sequence.

The little church bell was mounted just above the vestry door in an all too imposing, lichen-spattered granite housing. The bell swung on a pivot to which was attached a short length of steel cable. The cable led through a narrow metal ring and was ingeniously spliced onto to a length of hairy rope. The rope hung down inside the vestry and was pulled to toll the bell. The cable squealed against its containing ring, marking yet another victim to a willingness for martyrdom to the absence of grease.

The relative imminence of a church service was signalled by two sequences of bell tolling. The second sequence was intended to motivate the laggards who failed to heed the first. The first sequence ran from precisely a quarter to the hour to ten minutes to the hour, and the second commenced at five minutes to the hour and stopped just short of the stroke of the hour. A steady tolling of the bell, somewhere above the funereal but below a racy staccato, was the order of practice.

For a short period, James was delegated by the vicar to ring the church bell to call the faithful to worship. Once he became adept, he came to feel that some variation on an otherwise monotonous tolling theme was called for. To add variety, he first of all raised and lowered the rate of tolling. His inspiration was vested in the belief that if the bell tolled faster, then the approaching congregation would pick up their pace. James never owned a watch, and so, not unlike that curious date of Easter, the timing of the two sequences of bell tolling, which once or twice became three in his hands, were a moveable feast.

The variations played havoc with the churchgoing routines of Alice, Jessie and Fanny Fuzz Bush. They found themselves quite unable to deal with the uncertainty of how and when and in what order they might arrive at the Church door.

Perhaps it would not have mattered had not Wesslick, in concert with his sister Alice, also found himself inconvenienced by an irregular tolling schedule of the church bell. When the same experience came to be shared by Wesslick's churchwarden partner John, also a Rose Hill dweller and a gentleman not noted for his tolerance of choirboys' antics, James's bell-ringing career was abruptly terminated.

———

The end of bell ringing did not signify the end of James's association with the choir, however. That event came a little later, in the early autumn of a year at the specific time of the St Peter's Harvest Festival.

Harvest Festival was an exciting time at the church. Many kinds of fruit, vegetables, tinned goods, confectionery, flowers, branches of trees, sheaves of corn, crab pots, fishing nets and even sometimes a punt and sets of oars were donated or loaned to decorate and garland St Peter's. The congregation could then really sing in celebration of the fact that "God our maker doth [hopefully] provide, all our wants to be supplied".

At her bakery down near the bottom of Fore Street, Mrs Sherratt, even though her primary allegiance was to the Roscarrock Hill chapel, traditionally baked a huge loaf of bread in the form of a golden sheaf of corn to make a centrepiece for the St Peter's Harvest Festival display.

For the duration of the Harvest Festival, the boys who attended choir practices, Sunday school and Sunday services were likely to find themselves face to face in the path of temptation with more pieces of fruit than they had seen assembled anywhere in the entire year up to then. No matter that the fruit on display was dominated by apples and oranges, with an occasional pear thrown in here and there for good luck, it was all fruit, it was all absolutely edible and it was all within reach.

The Harvest Festival inevitably ended with a somewhat reduced inventory of the fruit that it had in place at the outset. Since no member of the choir or the Sunday school (or for that matter of the general congregation) would admit to having left church with a piece of fruit secreted on his or her person, it had to be assumed that God (or St Peter) had developed a sweet tooth.

———

It was usual for a large bunch of real grapes to be fixed to the front of the pulpit, from whence its glossy blue presence drew the attention of the boys like a magnet attracting iron filings. Grapes were as rare as bananas and were viewed by the boys as manna sent from heaven. In order that the bunch of grapes should not stray from the church in the manner of more than a few of the apples and oranges, it was woven with string to the wood of the pulpit by an expert in tying knots, evidently one who had received instructions from a fisherman. That probably meant that it wasn't the vicar who tied them.

What the vicar did overlook was that, secure though the bunch of grapes might be as a unit, individual grapes could be liberated from it with comparative ease. The plucking of grapes began cautiously enough, but soon gained a bolder momentum. There were more than a few choirboys both eager and anxious to sample this scarce and enticing treat.

By mid-week after Harvest Festival Sunday, not much more than the skeletal remains of the once proud bunch of grapes was left to glorify the front of the pulpit, Such grapes as did still hang onto the desiccated stalks were few and too mildewed even for a boy's taste.

———

James, who had an eye for such things, discovered that a quarter-pound bar of Cadbury's milk chocolate was secreted out of sight behind a large vegetable marrow on one of the windowsills in the nave of St Peters. It was a suitable place to hide the chocolate, as the windowsills were high enough above the floor to be out of reach of hands questing up from below. When James stood on a chair, however, he encountered no such problem.

Having located the milk chocolate, James was faced with the dreadful quandary of what to do about it. He knew that if he told anyone else where the chocolate was, the bar would very likely vanish within a rather short space of time. He went to check up on the chocolate a couple of times, and the fact that it remained undisturbed told him that apart from whoever had placed it behind the marrow on the window sill (presumably the vicar), and himself, no one else was in on the secret.

By Friday James's desire to sample the chocolate became compelling. Before heading off to the weekly cinema at the Rivoli, he entered the nave of St Peter's, pulled one of the chairs over to the wall below the relevant window, stood on the chair, grabbed the quarter-pound bar of chocolate, opened one end of it, broke off a couple of squares and ate them.

The taste of the chocolate was, in keeping with the general environment of where James stood, quite heavenly. Eating two more squares was called for.

What then remained of the chocolate bar didn't really seem worth returning to the windowsill. As the chocolate was not tied down like the grapes James put the remainder of the bar in his pocket, replaced the chair, left the church and walked up to the Rivoli with the contraband. Once inside the cinema, he broke up the rest of the squares of chocolate and shared them with his friends seated together on the sixpenny benches.

The vicar of the day was not the Rev. W. Atterbury Thomas, who had by then, to the regret of far too many, moved away to take up a new living. The vicar in the driving seat was the Rev. W. Atterbury Thomas's all too gung-ho successor, the Rev. F. B. Soady. The Rev. F. B. Soady may very well have been anticipating savouring the Harvest Festival chocolate bar himself. His attention to the chocolate was sure to have been as diligent as that of James, since he was in an incandescent rage when James met him in the vestry prior to Evensong on the following Sunday. The Rev. F. B.

Soady had not only noted the disappearance of the chocolate bar but had conducted an investigation, appointing himself policeman, arresting officer, judge, jury and executioner.

He learned from an informer, who may have been Rosie, the Rivoli's usher, that James had attended the cinema on the previous Friday with some chocolate on his person. Rosie was never wrong. The Rev. F. B. Soady determined that James was guilty of larceny from the House of God beyond any reasonable doubt.

The disappearance of grapes from the pulpit was an event that was usually glossed over. The removal of apples and oranges from the Harvest Festival display was accepted as inevitable. The theft of the bar of chocolate, in contrast, managed to touch a raw nerve in the person of the vicar. James forgave himself at once, but the Rev. F. B. Soady did not. James's illustrious membership of the choir was to be no more.

The last time that James met up with the Rev. F B. Soady was on the pathway between Front Hill and the church vestry. It was dark, although the hour was not late. The Rev. F. B. Soady came down the path with his wife, meeting James heading up. Mrs Soady remarked "Oh, look who's here!" The Rev. F. B. Soady lowered his head even further than he was accustomed to do in his normal stance and swept on by James without a word. Charity was not in the Rev. F. B. Soady's less than reverend heart on that evening.

The interior of St Peter's church

The St Peter's PT Club at the Duke of Cornwall's Light Infantry Barracks, Bodmin. In the back row and kneeling at the flanks of the second row are members of the DCLI fencing and judo teams

FROM LEFT TO RIGHT – *Front row:* John Welch, David Sherratt, CPO Arthur Welch, John Nown, Bruce Rowe, Charlie Rowe. *Second row:* Raymond Bate, Dennis Knight, Bryan Nicholls, Anthony Angell, Trevor Platt, Tommy Bradshaw *Third row:* Michael Bate, Roger Keat, James Platt, Tony Robinson, Robert May, Sydney Pluckrose.

11

The SPPTC

THE ST PETER'S PHYSICAL TRAINING CLUB was sometimes known as the SPPTC, but since even that abbreviation was still too much of a mouthful for the boys who were its members, they knew it more simply as "the PT Club".

The PT club counted boys of all ages from five to fifteen among its membership. It met once a week in the hall of the Church Rooms up at the top of Front Hill. Although the PT Club was indelibly associated with St Peter's church, Methodist Chapel boys were equally welcome to bridge the great religious divide and come along as members.

Boys who were Catholics or agnostics, or for that matter atheists, would also not be turned away from PT Club membership, although in order for them to join it would first of all be necessary to find one who belonged to those persuasions, as they were rare beasts.

The PT Club was founded by Chief Petty Officer Arthur Welch R.N. CPO Arthur, stationed at Devonport, lived at "Bay View" on the inside curve of lower Front Hill, appropriately enough right beneath the matt-backed, gothic gaze of the three stained glass windows that graced the back wall of St Peter's church.

CPO Arthur ran the PT Club under a regime of tight naval discipline. The PT Club was CPO Arthur's personal fiefdom. Although he was possibly a little too short and too round in stature to comply with the conventional image of a CPO on active duty, his sense of presence was enormous, and he radiated an aura of command. CPO Arthur symbolised power and dynamism. He led from the front and through example, treating one and all alike, and inspiring the boys with his firm benevolence.

—

The function of the PT Club as established by CPO Arthur was to develop teamwork and community spirit to replace the rough and ready ragged-assed individualism that characterised the boys and their usual run of activities. His overriding objective was to draw out and blend together the best personal qualities of all of the boys through their joint participation in co-ordinated physical training exercises.

CPO Arthur's dispensation of discipline to errant PT Club members came as and when it was due – no more, no less. His strong hand of discipline fell instantly and directly, but never unfairly. Any boys who felt the hard edge of CPO Arthur's iron will knew they had got exactly what their conduct deserved. They accepted it without rancour and moved on with a clean slate thereafter, unmarked by a single iota of resentment.

CPO Arthur encouraged the boys to do their best. The boys learned to their great advantage that when they did their best they became true achievers. Irrespective of whether or not they fell short of achieving the level of performance of others in doing so, their best gained the approbation of CPO Arthur.

—

However, CPO Arthur held a minimal tolerance for deliberate slackers and those who in his opinion "could do better". His pet hate was any owner of what he referred to as a "delay action brain". When CPO Arthur said, "Jump!" he meant, "Jump now!" So the boys jumped now.

CPO Arthur wanted crisp and co-ordinated movement. His measure of greatness was in causing such skills to bloom enthusiastically in the stony ground of PT Club membership. The boys were induced to pull together not only for CPO Arthur but also on their own account, not because he told them to do so but purely because they genuinely wanted to.

Following the inauguration of the PT Club, the order of physical training was vested mainly in group drilling and exercising, including stride jumping, push-ups, touching toes, arm and knee bends, balancing and head stands (with and without a chair, with and without varying degrees of success) and slinging a medicine ball to and fro.

The medicine ball was covered in stained leather and smelt of anguished sweat. Where it came from the boys didn't know and didn't want to know. It was heavy and squat, reputedly stuffed with horsehair. The bigger boys quickly learned that if they threw the medicine ball hard in the direction of one or other of the smaller boys, the result was rather satisfying.

As the skills of the PT Club matured and unified through steady practice, CPO Arthur extended both its range and repertoire of dedicated activities. One day a wooden sectioned vaulting horse appeared in the church rooms. It had a leather covered upholstered top. It was not clear if horsehair was again a feature of the upholstery.

Training on the wooden horse, the boys mastered through-jumps, stride-jumps, neck rolls and dive rolls. The fearsome short-arm back lift was another matter, but was also conquered eventually by a few of the boys through dogged persistence.

When in use for exercises, the wooden horse was always placed in the selfsame spot on the floor of the Church Rooms. It was not difficult to imagine certain individuals tunnelling out of the Church Rooms from beneath the wooden horse, heading for escape in the direction of Front Hill.

The wooden horse was then joined on the Church Rooms floor by a set of parallel bars. These were solid and unyielding.

As implements they were not for the unwary to tackle. Their use was restricted to the few articulately jointed members of the PT Club.

Indian clubs were equally lethal in the hands of the inexperienced. Their capacity for use as offensive weapons by PT Club members anxious to settle personal scores was not lost on CPO Arthur, and so their removal from service came not too long after their initial commission.

———

At an inspired moment, CPO Arthur determined that the PT Club had achieved a status calling for its light to be no longer hidden under a bushel. A public exhibition of PT Club talents was then arranged to take place in conjunction with the annual St Peter's church summer fête.

The public exhibition was received with great acclaim, and as a direct consequence the PT Club's reputation came to transcend the constraint of the parish boundary. The PT Club took up invitations to perform at village carnivals and fêtes outside Port Isaac in various parts of the surrounding district.

Using the wooden horse as the centrepiece, CPO Arthur designed some set pyramidal tableaux, in which the bigger boys provided the support at the base and the smallest boys were sent up to tremble in fear at the apex. The tableaux became popular and climactic features of PT Club exhibitions.

———

The original PT Club uniform was an unblemished white, assuming that an occasional grass stain could be ignored. It consisted of white vests, white shorts, white socks and heavily blancoed plimsolls that flaked and puffed at will as the most recent blanco application disintegrated consequent on exercises.

As the fame of the PT Club grew, some members of the St Peter's Mothers' Union under the imperial direction of the aptly named Mrs Angell, designed and embroidered a set of distinctive PT club badges consisting of the letters "SPPTC" interwoven in pale blue thread on a pale blue edged shield. The badges were sewn onto the boys' white vests, right in the centre of the breast.

To further enhance the scope of the PT Club, CPO Arthur introduced amateur boxing contests between selected, and presumably, although not necessarily, well-matched PT club members. The boxing went on to become, for the general public, the PT Club's most anticipated activity.

The PT Club boxing ring was constructed from four corner poles with two strands of relatively tight rope strung around it. The boxing gloves were sixteen ounce size and, when fitted, gave certain of the smaller exponents of the so-called "noble art" something of the appearance of a big-handed character from one of the full supporting programme cartoons which were sometimes shown at the Rivoli cinema.

The participating boxers might in some cases have been less than happy to don the gloves and step into the ring, but, with CPO Arthur as the promoter in charge, their option was that of Whitaker in "The Red Planet", the second in the famous series of *Journey Into Space* wireless serials by Charles Chilton. According to Whittaker, "Orders must be obeyed without question at all times." There was room neither for retreat nor for surrender.

As was the case with so many of the good things in life, CPO Arthur, under the pressure of naval duties, moved away from Port Isaac eventually, to the deep dismay not only of PT Club members but also of the host of those who, far and wide, were touched by what he had done for them.

Yet, oddly enough, for a while after the departure of CPO Arthur, the PT Club, under CPO Arthur's successor Mr Melvyn Watkins, seemed to gain in strength, bolstered by an increased focus on boxing. Melvyn was known as "Taffy". He was blessed with a Welsh accent fluid enough to paddle a canoe on.

The PT Club undertook boxing tournaments against other

North Cornish youth clubs, some as far away as Bude and Launceston. A boxing tournament always filled the Church Rooms to capacity with spectators.

———

For all that, CPO Arthur's loss was a body blow to the PT Club. The final outcome for the PT Club without CPO Arthur was never really in doubt.

The inspirational glue that held the PT club together went into an inevitable decay, the light faded and a once gloriously active institution became no more than a cherished memory.

The SPPTC poised in its show-stopping final tableau

Downtown Port Isaac from the Pentice (left) to Roscarrock Hill (right)

12

The Fruiterer

MR ALTAIR BUNT'S SHOP stood, fronted by a narrow stretch of pavement, directly across from the Pentice on the inner flank of Fore Street. Mr Altair Bunt's house adjoined the shop on the downhill side. The far wall of his house lay along the bottom edge of Rose Hill.

The Pentice was characterised by a wall, maybe a foot and a half thick, four feet high and thirty feet long. The wall was built up from chunks of slate of various dimensions, no two of which were alike. Its rounded capping was formed from more regularly sorted pieces of slate laid on end and mortared together.

The rounded capping evolved partly by design, and probably more substantially through the wear and tear of generations of elbows and folded arms that had been placed on it as their owners gossiped, leaned over and contemplated the prospect of the inner harbour that greeted them. The Pentice was as important a locality for social contact as was Little Hill, further up Fore Street.

The Pentice wall incidentally formed a link along the harbour-side edge of Fore Street between the sunken front of Harry and Olive Bate's house and the back living quarters of the Golden Lion. Its presence offered the assurance that no passing pedestrian need fall over into the harbour in front of Mr Altair Bunt's shop unless he or she really wanted to.

From the outer side of the Pentice wall a steep roof of tarry slates fell away towards the harbour, covering a rising terrace of fishermen's cellars. Gulls paraded on the roof and strutted the length of the wall, waiting to see if someone would feed them with a few scraps. They were rarely disappointed.

———

Mr Altair Bunt was part and parcel of the Pentice scene, although he tended to observe it from the safe confines of his shop. He was not an especially popular man with the general public, but that was all right because courting popularity was not in his nature. He was known to one and all by the familiar but hardly affectionate name of "Tair", or more likely "Old Tair", the latter being as near enough a match to Altair as anyone would wish to make.

Old Tair was neither fleshy nor thin. His shoulders were stooped, and he held them poised as if he were expecting a stick to be brought down across them at any moment. There were a considerable number of Port Isaac residents who might have been ready to fulfil Old Tair's expectations, had they but been bolder.

Old Tair's hair was as thin as his smile on even a good day. He peered at his customers with critical eyes over a bulbous, slightly hooked nose, summing them up, giving them the impression that he was a man who knew their darker secrets.

———

In Port Isaac circles a secret, especially a dark one, was something that everyone knew about and pretended they didn't. Those who lived in glasshouses were not really in any position to throw stones, but even the hint of a secret provided an advantage for all that, and when an advantage was needed the glasshouse could shatter where it would.

———

Old Tair invariably wore a long brown dustcoat when serving in his shop. His dustcoat was not quite as loosely flowing as those which the boys once saw Jesse and Frank James wearing in a big film at the Rivoli cinema, but they weren't slow to draw an appropriate association between Old Tair and Jesse as a consequence.

Such an association was only enhanced by the fact that Old

Tair wore a thin gold ring in the lobe of his right ear. If the boys were to be asked, even though they never were, to specify the single feature of Old Tair that most impressed them, they would have cited Old Tair's gold earring. They linked the earring with pirates and piracy. The earring ensured that for the boys Old Tair was one to watch out for. Old Tair did nothing to dispel this reputation.

———

Above the scarred entry door to Old Tair's shop, a peeling sign carried the unique legend, "A. Bunt, Fruiterer". The title of "Fruiterer" probably raised the curiosity of customers as to what "Fruiterer" meant, rather than the expectation of what might be on sale inside the shop. Any expectations were doomed to failure in any case, since perhaps the most memorable characteristic of Old Tair's shop was the limited amount of fresh produce of any kind on display.

Within the shop, perpetual twilight made itself at home and dwelt supreme. The atmosphere hung like smoke under a resigned sense of gloom that would not have been unfamiliar to Mr Ebeneezer Scrooge, preferably played by the great actor Alastair Sim. As a customer came in through the shop door, Old Tair was usually over there on the right, lurking about in the dimness at a dingy wooden counter set up alongside a curtained door leading into his house.

On the wall behind the counter a long dead pocket watch was gibbeted on a nail. Underneath the watch a piece of yellowing paper was prevented from fluttering to the floor by a strategically applied drawing pin. A handwritten slogan on the piece of paper read. "No tick here". Old Tair had a sense of humour of which Scrooge would also have approved.

Directly facing customers coming into Old Tair's shop was a wooden display rack. It appeared to have been assembled in a hurry and without regard for its longevity. The rack did its level – or more correctly, slightly askew – best to garner as much sustenance as it could from such light as managed to filter in through the grimy glass of the shop door.

On top of the wooden rack sat some large glass jars containing boiled sweets, anxiously awaiting the arrival of ration books from which Old Tair snipped out the coupons with a pair of long scissors. The scissors may have been sharp, but they were not nearly as sharp as Old Tair.

———

Old Tair was never less than consistent in his application of weights and measures. Each customer received the precise weight that the laws of rationing decreed, no more and no less. Old Tair was known to break up boiled sweets as a guarantee that the statutory two ounces would not be exceeded.

———

In season, on a lower shelf of the wooden rack, a basket of apples was on display. Their presence might have been used to justify Old Tair's title of "Fruiterer". The appearance of the apples – green, scabbed, and roundabout rather than round – could have been described as unappealing without fear of contradiction.

The stock of Old Tair's shop additionally featured tinned goods in a number of varieties, although falling a long way short of the magic number of fifty-seven. Dried eggs were also available, and there were, importantly, bundles of candles and boxes of matches. Old Tair's cigarette inventory was shut away in a drawer behind the shop counter.

———

Candles were greatly prized by those boys who were enthusiastic explorers of caves and abandoned mine adits. Sometimes the boys were able to expropriate a candle stump or two from home, since most households kept a few candles stuck in a drawer somewhere. The candles were taken out following the onset of power cuts in cottages connected up to electricity, or for illuminating the way to bed when the oil lamps were turned out in those cottages that were not yet electrically powered.

When all alternatives for the boys to acquire candles failed, however, Old Tair's stock of candles was there to be taken advantage of. The problem was that Old Tair was entirely averse to selling candles to any of the boys.

———

As Old Tair rationalised it, candles were designed to be lit. Lighting a candle required a match to be struck. Matches were used to fire up cigarettes. Candles, matches, cigarettes and boys made an unbalanced equation in Old Tair's book of calculations. Old Tair undertook to ensure, by all means in his not inconsiderable power, that any means of lighting up anything was kept well out of any so-called under-age grasp.

———

Old Tair was of course happy, or as happy as he ever was, to sell prescribed quantities of cigarettes, without hesitation, to those legally qualified to smoke. Smoking was a universal habit, greatly enjoyed by its practitioners, who as often as not hated themselves for enjoying it so much. Would-be smoking practitioners, who were unable by reason of age to practice the art, saw their first drag at a fag as a major goal to be achieved in life.

Picking up fag ends in the street was one means of beating the system, but it was laborious and the gleanings were small as there were few smokers who threw down fag ends containing much residual tobacco. The acquisition of a first real fag by the boys was anticipated with a similar level of excitement to that accompanying their first pair of long trousers.

———

Any attempt by a boy to buy a candle from Old Tair, with or without accompanying matches, therefore resulted in his instant denunciation by Old Tair. Moreover Old Tair would then order the boy, in tones of considerable ferocity, to vacate his shop immediately. Old Tair's tirade did not cease with the hurried departure of the boy, but rattled in hot pursuit down Fore Street after him.

———

The boys deemed it essential to resort to alternative methods to acquire a much-needed candle from Old Tair. One option was to tell Old Tair that the candle was being purchased either for Tom Brown, the manager of Pawlyn's Cellars, or for the Port Isaac harbourmaster, Anthony Provis. Old Tair was not always inclined to question the nomination of such prominent local personalities as his customers.

There were lots of precedents in any case for boys running errands to Old Tair for Tom and Anthony and other regulars around the Town Platt. They all took great delight in sending the boys up to Old Tair, not to mention to certain other shopkeepers in Fore Street, to enquire about the availability of a left handed screwdriver, or a tin of black and white striped paint, or a hole to hang on Pawlyn's cellar wall in order that those on the inside would be able to see what the weather was like on the outside.

If the "Tom Brown sent us up" scheme failed, as it often did, the fallback action was a mass invasion of Old Tair's shop by a gang of boys. While a couple of them distracted Old Tair's attention, the others would try to surreptitiously pocket a candle, or half a candle was equally acceptable, together with a couple of red-headed matches from a box of "England's Glory".

"England's Glory" matches would strike a light on almost any rough surface. The matches were slipped out of a matchbox picked up from the pile on display, while the practitioner of the sleight of hand conducted the pretext of reading the joke printed on the back of the box.

A matchbox joke was a timeless classic of true distinction, and when the boys came to think about it, so probably was Old Tair.

The east wall and head of Port Isaac harbour from the school on the left around to the Town Platt and Harbour Café on the right

Khandalla, Northcliff and the rise of Lobber Field, Port Isaac

13

The Battle of Roscarrock Hill

THE IDEAL LOCATION from which to obtain a ringside view of Roscarrock Hill was at Little Hill on Fore Street.

Little Hill was a sun-drenched nook located on the right hand side of Fore Street over from Chapman's grocer's shop. It was a popular meeting place for the exchange of gossip. Two public benches were supplied for those who wished to tarry awhile at Little Hill when the flow of gossip was too good to interrupt.

One of the Little Hill public benches was set flat against the back wall of the out around area of the school playground. Anyone seated on that bench could look towards as much of down town Port Isaac as was not obscured by the public lavatory wall that formed the boundary of Little Hill on its lower side.

The other public bench stood at right angles to its companion, its back precisely parallel to the descending line of Fore Street behind it. This bench commanded a view over a low wall that was built up from slabs of slate and was doing its best to hold fast on the very edge of the cliff that dropped away fifty feet or more on the outside to the harbour beach.

From this second bench the view took in most of the harbour and pretty much all of Roscarrock Hill, running up from Pawlyn's and Roscarrock chapel at the bottom to the stately building named "Khandalla" sheltered in under the glowing curve of Lobber field at the top.

The dominant features of the upper part of Roscarrock Hill, apart from the fact that those responsible for its surface maintenance had yet to agree on what to do and when, if ever, to do it, were the tall house named Northcliff, standing as erect as a white exclamation mark on the verge of an elegant sweep of cliffside allotments, and a gaunt, brick-edged mansion standing in perpetual shadow on a damp-backed terrace over behind Northcliff.

The latter was the property of Captain Roy May (Retired Army). Roy was the owner of significant property around Port Isaac. Whatever his income was, or might have been, Roy's gone-to-seed appearance suggested that he used (or had used) either little or none of his alleged fortune to purchase soap. He grew potatoes in a little garden on the downhill side of Northcliff, although some of the Port Isaac born said that Roy could as well have grown the tetties in the grime occupying the creases of his neck.

The appearance of the interior of Roy's mansion was rumoured to have much in common with Launceston jail. Launceston (or "Lanson") jail was a by-word for disorderliness. The Port Isaac boys, to whom Roy showed no shred of benevolence, might be forgiven for having compared Roy's decaying mansion with an edifice called the House of Usher that fell down in a story one of the boys once read.

———

Roy's immediate downhill neighbours on Roscarrock Hill were Mr Teddy Hosking and his wife Mary. Teddy was familiarly known as "Teddy Bush". Their principal residence was a chunky, two-storey cottage built of raw slate and edged around with red brickwork. However, the couple chose not to dwell in this cottage, preferring to let it out to holiday tenants. So as not to be too far removed from their property, however, Teddy Bush and Mary lived on a hillside terrace above the cottage in two little wooden shacks, from which vantage point they could look down on the cottage roof and beyond it across the harbour to the school, Little Hill, the descent of Fore Street and the ever-rising backing jumble of the bulk of Port Isaac.

———

Teddy Bush was an elderly ex-seaman, only a little overweight. He had wild, wispy hair and a bulbous nose from which a pendulous dewdrop swung perpetually. His teeth were few and brown and leaned about in his mouth like weathered slate flags rimming a disused quarry. In his manner of dress Teddy Bush invariably wore a battered sailor's cap with a once shiny visor, a threadbare double-breasted black suit jacket a couple of sizes too large for him, and trousers which were originally grey and which served to disprove the local adage that grey tended not to show the dirt.

———

Teddy Bush was a brother to Mr Jackie Hosking, another former seafarer. Jackie lived in a tight little cottage in a narrow ope leading up to Rose Hill from the side of Sherratt's bakery. He was an affable gentleman in manner, seldom seen without a fired-up pipe firmly clenched between his teeth. Jackie was married to Annie, who, coincidentally if not curiously, was a sister to Teddy Bush's Mary.

———

Teddy Bush and Mary had the misfortune not to be blessed with children. Jackie and Annie by contrast had two boys, William and Arthur. William Hosking was nicknamed "Gaggy", or sometimes "Willie Gaggy". Most Port Isaac people would have been hard pressed to place who William Hosking was, but the name Gaggy Hosking promoted instant recognition.

Gaggy was so-called because of his propensity to be unreliable, which was a lot more than alleged. He had a great talent for taking liberties with the truth, being able to promise anything and deliver nothing, even though he undoubtedly meant everything he said, when he said it. Beyond that, in the track of time, Gaggy moved on, his promises evaporating behind him like the penny-sized raindrops of an April shower plopped on a warm road.

Gaggy was of average height and average build. There was a lot that was average about him. His most distinguishing feature was his light coloured, naturally wavy hair. It gave him something of the look of a young Spencer Tracy. If he was not a lovable rogue, he was certainly a likeable member of the rogue species. It was impossible not to feel a fondness for Gaggy.

Those who knew Gaggy well could readily adjust to the illusions he created, could look on him with tolerance and forbearance and could generally admire his natural ability to flounder through the tide of life against steady waves of discouragement and never quite sink.

Gaggy spent much more of his time in the company of Teddy Bush and Mary than he did in that of Jackie and Annie. Mary came to be called "Mother Mary" by him, as if providing Gaggy with a direct reflection of the part he perceived Mary to play in his life.

———

Mother Mary's width was very nearly twice that of Teddy Bush. She was big muscled and strong-armed into the bargain and was very loud voiced. In her style of dress she favoured bright floral frocks with sleeves loose enough to leave her arms free for lifting objects that could be thrown, commonly in the direction of Teddy Bush. Should Teddy Bush be unavailable, there was always the option of Gaggy to make an equally acceptable target for Mother Mary.

If Gaggy was also elsewhere when combat called, Mother Mary's fallback was the resurrection from its unsealed casket of a shouting row conducted with Annie. This conflict between the sisters married to the brothers had no good sustaining cause that anyone could remember. It had maintained a sequence of eruptions for so long, however, that it had become a matter of resigned routine. Family feuds in Port Isaac tended to spring like mighty trees from roots of staggering triviality. Two brothers marrying two sisters established almost the perfect recipe for the release of turbulence.

———

Annie might have made a marginally trimmer figure than Mother Mary, but she gave back at least as good as she got from her sister. She enjoyed the sibling rows just as much as Mother Mary did. Annie was at her very best when blasting a stream of invective along the lower part of Fore Street at the wobbling rear of a rapidly retreating Mother Mary.

It was not out of the question for Mother Mary and Annie to continue "hollin' and shoutin'" at each other as Mother Mary distanced herself from Annie down past the Town Platt and up along the length of Roscarrock Hill. The exchanges easily bridged the harbour. Jackie puffed away at his pipe and placidly sat it all out, having heard it all many times previously. Arthur, a stable man who took after Jackie in temperament, was sometimes called in to mediate between Mother Mary and Annie if the conflict of words lasted longer than was absolutely necessary.

Within the spit and sawdust public bar sector of the Golden Lion it was alleged that Annie in full cry in Fore Street was able to induce bottles of St Austell Light Ale to chink against each other on the pub shelves. There was also no doubt that the barrels of beer shivered against the side wedges that held them level, in sympathy with the bottles. Pint sinkers shuddered and took a deep suck of the flat brew in their glasses to convince themselves that their draught mild and bitter, almost a synonym for Jackie and Annie, had not reacted to Annie's tones by turning sour.

The most magnificent battles fought within the Hosking family were not battles of words, however. They were rather those features of legendary vehemence and full Technicolor starring Teddy Bush and Mother Mary on their Roscarrock Hill property, acted out in full view of the very many enthusiastic spectators drawn to Little Hill to marvel at the spectacle. Even with the distance across the harbour separating the spectators from the action, the clarity of the diction with which Teddy Bush and Mother Mary bawled insults in each other's direction made for an easy sound track to follow.

The two wooden huts were pivotal to the strategy of enactment of the regular wars between Teddy Bush and Mother Mary. These two principal combatants stood like bookends, one against each of the far ends of the respective cabins, both screaming continuous abuse and sporadically emerging from cover to hurl missiles at one another.

The missiles were stones, clods of earth, chunks of wood or any other object big enough to grab, solid enough to grip and not so heavy that it could not be heaved hard in the right direction.

None of the spectators really knew why these battles took place. It was enough that they did. It seemed to take very little to set them off. Gaggy was rarely very far away when the real action commenced, and, although it was never proved conclusively, he gained a reputation as a master catalyst provoking at least some of the conflict.

———

Avoiding lines of fire, Gaggy alternated his allegiance between Teddy Bush and Mother Mary to ensure that each had a ready supply of assault material well to hand. The combat continued until one or other of the antagonists in these brilliant set pieces came into direct contact with one of the other party's projectiles. Since Mother Mary had the surer aim, Teddy Bush was tailor-made as the object for the decisive strike.

Honour having been satisfied, an instant truce broke out. Teddy Bush and Mary, naturally enough plus Gaggy, then linked arms and strolled down Roscarrock Hill to go and visit Jackie and Annie. Teddy Bush as often as not would be decorated by a thin red line of blood trickling down one of his whiskery cheeks, dripping in unrepentant glory onto the outsize lapels of his jacket.

———

Gaggy was no doubt already thinking about the following round, planning in advance for the next campaign.

Mr Teddy "Bush" Hosking

Granfer Jim Creighton and James Platt
at the front door of 7 Canadian Terrace

14

The Best of the "R"s

JAMES CONSIDERED HIMSELF to be fortunate to be able to grow up surrounded by committed readers of books. Books formed a key essential of life support for both his Gran and his Granfer Creighton as well as for his mother.

———

The exception that proved this rule was his father, who had little interest in books, although his father did own one book, namely a leather bound copy of *The Pilgrim's Progress*, with which he was presented on the occasion of his joining the Royal Navy, back before the war that was. That copy of the masterwork by John Bunyan was in such pristine condition that no eye, let alone any thumb might ever have rested on any one of its flimsy India paper pages. *The Pilgrims Progress* resided on the top shelf of an airing cupboard, resting comfortably under a pile of sheets that its author might well have been grateful for in the jail where he wrote the book.

By the time that James's father returned home, demobilised through ill-health after the war, James had already been reading avidly for a couple of years, so there was then no example his father could show him that could mar his further progress.

———

His mother read, almost exclusively, novels of romance, otherwise known as "love" books. Gran Creighton lapped up crime and "detective" stories; and Granfer Creighton ploughed through a never-ending posse of western yarns.

Granfer's love of slim volumes involving cowhands, fist fights, gunplay and a marginal romantic interest that only made its appearance somewhere near the back cover, was quite equal to that of Tom Brown, the manager of Pawlyn's fish cellars. Tom was particularly addicted to the western novels of Clarence E. Mulford, featuring the personage of Hopalong Cassidy. Tom's vegetable garden, located a short way out in the Port Isaac valley, adjacent to the stream, was named for Hopalong's outfit, the "Bar 20" ranch. The name "Bar 20" was picked out in rope on a board mounted above the garden gate.

Hopalong Cassidy films, starring the immortal Bill Boyd clad in spotless black, were frequently featured up at the Rivoli cinema, but neither Bill's acting prowess nor that of Bill's garrulous old timer sidekick, invariably played by Gabby Hayes, ever proved magnetic enough to draw Tom or Granfer to performances.

Suffice it to say that for them, the arrival of the travelling lending library at its regular stopping place in Fore Street beside the school railings, across from the Old Drug Store, was a much more eagerly anticipated weekly event.

It seemed to James that wherever he was in 6 Canadian Terrace, where he lived, and next door in 7 Canadian Terrace, where Gran and Granfer lived, there were books for him to trip over, garish, vividly coloured dust jackets to look at, and pages full of tightly packed words to ponder over.

A book jacket that impressed itself deeply on him covered one of his Gran's detective novels entitled *Wake not the Sleeping Wolf*, written by Mr Trent McCoy. The picture on the jacket was of a shadowy, hulking figure looking across a deserted, rain-swept street in which stood only a darkened police car. The legend underneath gave advice to the would-be reader that "*Organised crime takes a beating when a private eye muscles in*".

That picture, above all others, caught James's imagination. It became vital to him to understand the associated legend. He was not yet able to read the words, but he could look at the letters, see their form and relate their patterns to the way they sounded when Gran spoke them. From that point it was just a short step for him to identify similar patterns of letters, words and the way they sounded elsewhere in other books.

James didn't remember exactly when the letters gathered together into words and the words into sentences that he could read. It just happened, as if a switch was thrown in his head. One day he ran his eyes over a page and heard the words on the page being spoken behind his eyes. All of a sudden, James could read, although he didn't tell anyone right away.

———

The box of porridge oats that faced James on the table at most breakfast times immediately became a readable item. He didn't have porridge for breakfast every day, actually preferring the alternative of bread and milk, but he had no choice in the matter when the porridge turned up.

He looked at the porridge box and read to himself what he saw written on it. James found out that the words he read told him how good the contents of the box were for him. He didn't believe that for a minute. It was a first lesson in the power of the written word to deceive.

———

James was then not far beyond his third birthday. His ability to read created a minor sensation. He developed the talent of reading so well that he was able to read fluently by the age of four from any book or newspaper, applying all required stress and punctuation. As a consequence he came to be regarded by many as something of a curiosity. On no small number of occasions he was placed on a chair too high for him to easily escape from in front of an unbelieving group, invariably of ladies, and was handed a book selected and opened at random for him to read a passage from.

On completion of the reading, the ladies made comments of the nature of "Isn't it marvellous!" as if James (or it) was some kind of performing dog. He was then free to flee from the circle of grudging admirers and the aura of face powder, tobacco and imperfectly suppressed sweat that surrounded it.

———

Gran and Granfer Creighton subscribed to a "sensible" daily newspaper, the *Daily Mail,* and its equally staid Sunday companion the *Sunday Dispatch.* Both of these added grist to James's reading mill. Sundays also saw Gran and Granfer taking the *News of the World,* although that was a newspaper James was not permitted to read in their presence.

When James did get to sneak a look at the *News of the World,* he wondered what the fuss was all about. The ponderous obliqueness that the *News of the World* brought to its reporting of the fall from grace of assorted clergymen, professional men and travelling salesmen read to him like extended clues for a difficult crossword puzzle.

James liked the *Daily Mail* for its comic strips, which he cut out every day and compiled in sequence, sticking them in scrapbooks using a paste made from flour and water. "Teddy Tail" related the adventures of an engaging, well-dressed mouse and his companions. "Rip Kirby" was a very well drawn and excellently plotted comic strip relating cases undertaken and solved by a bespectacled, lean-jawed private detective. "Rufus", who was regularly upstaged by his friend named "Flook", looking like a cross between a soft teddy bear and an elephant, provided James with enormous entertainment.

———

James graduated rapidly from the comics for the very young, *Rainbow* and *Tiny Tots* among them, to get into the vastly more satisfying fare of the *Beano* and the *Dandy.* The *Beano* and the *Dandy* were published fortnightly, reflecting the persistence of wartime restrictions on paper supplies that had also slimmed down the daily newspapers.

With access to the *Beano* and the *Dandy* James revelled in the antics of comic characters of the calibre of Korky the Kat and Big Eggo the ostrich; Lord Snooty and his pals; Keyhole Kate; Hungry Horace; Tom Thumb; Desperate Dan; Jimmy and his Magic Patch; Black Bob the Scottish sheepdog; and Strang the Terrible. Strang the Terrible, James's favourite, clad in a leopard skin, was infinitely more exciting in jungle adventures than Tarzan could ever have dreamed of being.

The *Beano* and *Dandy* were wonderful comics: crisp, exciting, and funny at the turn of every page. They combined pictures in the ideal way with printed words. Very many of the Port Isaac boys cut their reading teeth on these treasures and were forever enriched thereafter.

Since James's birthday fell in August, and the school year began in September, it meant that he was destined to be the youngest member of his class by anything up to a year. He commenced school in the month after his fourth birthday at a class in the Church Rooms taken by the saintly Miss Dawe.

The facilities of the County Primary school in Fore Street had been unable to cope with the great influx of children evacuated during the war to the comparative safety of Port Isaac from the danger of the cities where they lived, and the consequent over-flow occupied the Church Rooms just as effectively as if it had been planned by Hitler.

When he became five years old, James left Miss Dawe and the Church Rooms and went down to the infants' class in the real school, where Miss Smythe taught him. Under her wings, James's reading went into full flight. By the time he was forced to leave Miss Smythe at the age of seven to enter the less than gentle clutches of Mrs Morman in the next class up, James had worked

147

through all the sequence of primary reading books from *Book One* to *Book Six*, and was at least three books ahead of the rest of his class, not that it made a lot of difference to Mrs Morman.

He had additionally read a number of Miss Smythe's personal books that she kept in a glass-fronted dresser in the infants' classroom. It included a book on bird identification, providing him with a firm scientific foundation for his subsequent activities in collecting birds' eggs.

———

James was able to recall and repeat whatever he read, which made him useful as a storyteller. A group of the bigger boys would often come and ask him to tell them a story, and he was happy to sit down on a Fore Street doorstep, or in a corner of the school playground, and to repeat to them what he had read in the latest comic or most recent book.

———

Miss Smythe introduced James to the works of Enid Blyton. He regularly read Enid's little pocket-sized magazine *Sunny Stories*, in which he especially liked stories about the Faraway Tree and Josie, Click and Bun. Enid's "Famous Five" and "Adventure" series, each presenting a group of children who became involved by accident in various forms of skulduggery and by doing so solved crimes, saved situations and turned themselves into heroes of the moment, provided hours of excitement. This was in spite of the fact that such children came from an upper class world in which primary schools seemed not to exist.

An unfortunate line was drawn however through Enid giving her characters names like Julian and Jeremy. The response of Port Isaac boys to the appearance of others bearing these distinctive names would echo that of two characters in a classic nineteenth-century *Punch* cartoon set in the "Mining Districts". One of the two advised his companion that he had spotted a toff, and the other responded "'Eave 'arf a brick at 'im".

———

James read as many of the "William" stories by Richmal Crompton as he could get his hands on. William was a different kettle of fish from the Julians and Jeremys who inhabited the world of Enid Blyton. William was an indomitable boy with a refreshingly common attitude, even though he was born into an over-pretentious family.

James looked eagerly in the *Radio Times* each week for announcements of *Just William* episodes to be broadcast on the wireless in Children's Hour, and whenever one was due, he settled back, always in Gran Creighton's sitting room, to enjoy every second of the half hour that followed William's mother's insistent call "*Williaaaaaaaam!*" followed by William's resigned rejoinder, "*All right mother, I'm coming!*". James was well able to relate to that.

———

James was not a regular listener to Children's Hour, as he found the delivery of the main presenters Derek McCulloch ("Uncle Mac") and David Davis ("David") to be too insipid for his taste, but *Just William* was not to be missed under any circumstances. Similar considerations applied to episodes featuring the cases of *Norman and Henry Bones, the boy detectives*, and to *Toytown*, based on stories written by S. G. Hulme Beaman.

The great character in *Toytown* was Larry the Lamb, who was himself played by none other than Uncle Mac. Larry's great antagonist was the irascible Mr Growser. James knew a number of people in Port Isaac who would not have been miscast in playing Mr Growser's role.

———

Novels, dealing with the adventures of boys at moments of great historical significance and in circumstances of considerable danger in exotic places, were always welcome reads. James's particular favourite of this genre was by the author Geo. Manville Fenn. Entitled *Cormorant Crag*, it was an adventure involving smuggling on a steep and rocky coast that James could easily imagine himself involved in.

———

Compendium volumes such as *Fifty Great Detective Stories*, and *Fifty Tales of Mystery and Imagination* were much in vogue at the time and were appreciably easy to skim through. They all seemed, true to their titles, to contain exactly fifty stories, no more and no less. Such volumes were heavy enough to drop on and flatten a rat.

Roger Keat lent James *Fifty Greatest Rogues, Tyrants and Criminals*, which James read from cover to cover. In doing so he discovered that in that particular copy of the book only forty-nine greatest rogues, tyrants and criminals were included. The fiftieth of the sorry gang, "Messalina, the Illustrious Harlot", incidentally the last chapter of the book, had been excised forever by the censorious scissors of Roger's Aunt Mary Bate.

———

Gran Creighton owned a severely tattered copy of *Blomfield's Martyrs*, published in 1809. Granfer told James that he had read the book from leather-bound cover to leather-bound cover. This was a mammoth feat of reading, but then Granfer had also read the whole Bible in a similarly complete manner.

Blomfield's Martyrs was little read by James, but it was much studied. Its pictures of impending death and torture were so undeniably bloodthirsty that he often wondered what Aunt Mary Bate might have made of them.

———

From the moment that the scales fell from James's eyes and printed words began to run in his head, he ached to own what he called a "thick book". A thick book was a book of the type that grown-ups read. It was hard-covered, compact, contained no pictures and was filled with a great wealth of pages that would turn in his hand with a rich creaminess. A thick book was something much nobler than the thinner but larger format books that were his standard fodder, although, come to think of it, the latter included the much valued *Beano Book* every year, and that was always a consolation.

James was hoping that his end of year Sunday school prize, handed out at the Sunday school Christmas party in the Church Rooms in December of the year after the war ended, would fulfil his thick book dream. Disappointingly the opportunity was dashed to pieces when a copy of *Saints who Spoke English* by Joan Windham, in format Demy 8vo, was handed over to James at the prize giving by the vicar, the Rev. W. Atterbury Thomas. The vicar was beaming. James was not.

It fell to Gran Creighton to buy James his first thick book. The book arrived on Christmas day in the following year. When James woke up, at an appropriately early hour, there was the thick book to be discovered, weighing down the bottom of the pillowcase hanging from the end of his bed. This was his dream come true, up to the time that he came to read the book that is.

The book was bound with a plain maroon hard cover. Its dust jacket, had it ever existed, didn't exist any longer. The story was not memorable. It featured a boy named Merry, a name at some odds with the turgid nature of the prose. However, it was a thick book, it was his and so James read it from cover to cover before he put it aside and never referred to it again.

———

If there was a benefit to be obtained from the thick book about the less than adventurous exploits of Merry, it was obtained from the "Contents" page. James's mother taught him that "Contents" was an abbreviation of "Cows Ought Not To Eat Nasty Turnip Skins". Better still, read in reverse, "Contents" signified that "Sam Took Nellie Every Tuesday Night Out Courting".

———

Although James never really abandoned the *Beano* and the *Dandy* as required reading material, he also took particular pleasure in reading boys' story papers, favouring the so-called *Big Four*.

This giant quartet of imaginative literature, each costing tuppence per issue, consisted of *Adventure* and *The Wizard* (billed by its publishers Messrs. D. C. Thompson & Co. as "the paper for a good long read"), both of which came out on Tuesdays, and *The Rover* and *The Hotspur*, which were available on Thursdays.

A fifth boys' story paper, *The Champion*, was also generally a good read, but never quite matched up to the style and quality of D. C. Thompson's Big Four, in James's opinion. *The Champion* came out on Fridays, in its case at a price of three pence. That extra penny was an important consideration in deciding which paper to buy.

The boys' story papers contained twelve pages of dingy print of the type that was used for the daily newspapers. There was no gloss involved. The only colours, other than the muted yellowish brown that stole across the pages under the grip of time, appeared on the front covers. The palette of colours that was applied fell some way short of being comparable to a rainbow.

The cover pages of *The Hotspur* and *The Champion* normally drew dramatic attention to an instant of considerable excitement in one of the stories that lay within. *Adventure* ran a crudely drawn strip cartoon on its cover, while *The Rover*, on its cover page, chose to present an array of school and sports club badges submitted by readers. The cover of *The Wizard* carried a hugely funny comic strip dealing with the antics of a tribe of natives overseen by "the Captain" and a boy named "Spadger" who had, inexplicably, been shipwrecked on an island named after Spadger.

The inside pages of the story papers were jam packed with tight columns of text in fine print, occasionally relieved by a small black and white sketch. Five or six stories were offered in each issue. Some of the stories were one-off yarns; others were serials with cliffhanger endings. Many of the stories involved characters that came to be counted as familiar friends by regular readers.

Depending on the season, at least one story with a football or cricketing association was included. Not the least famous among these were "Baldy Hogan's Bullseyes", "Willie Wallop", "It's goals that count", and "It's wickets that count", (or alternatively "It's runs that count").

There were wonderful stories about athletes, involving the timeless classic "Truth about Wilson" and "Alf Tupper, the Tough of the Track"; about school, as with "Red Circle", and "Smith of the Lower Third"; the wild west, notable examples being "Solo Solomon", "The Eyes of the Blind Outlaw", and "Slade of the Pony Express"; the war, with "Rockfist Rogan", and "I flew with Braddock"; mystery and detection in which Dixon Hawke was king; jungle adventures featuring Strang the Terrible and Morgyn the Mighty; and a vast host of historical, futuristic and "specialist" adventures into the bargain.

The principal ingredients common to the whole feast of tales were action, thrills, fun, humour and imagination.

———

The stories of the life, tribulations and invariable success of Wilson, which appeared in *The Wizard*, were among the most universally popular. Wilson was an immortal. Born in the eighteenth century, he had been immersed in the fountain of youth. The drawback he faced was that in order to retain his immortality he was required to re-immerse himself in the same fountain every so often, and Wilson not infrequently played his rejuvenation technique close to the line. Wilson was the quintessential athlete, performing always in a black single-piece leotard.

———

Each of the Big Four had its own distinctive style and flavour. It was only necessary for James to dip into a given story to know instantly which of the Big Four it had come from. *The Wizard* carried what was probably the most serious of all the writing presented. Its tales were literate and absorbing. *The Rover* endeavoured to present a serious front as well, but ended up being rather po-faced instead.

Adventure and *The Hotspur* offered lighter reading, specialising in school stories that were both exciting and funny, a world of clean cut types where good always triumphed. The schools in the stories were almost invariably boarding schools, well outside the experience of Port Isaac boys, but that didn't matter at all to the enjoyment.

The common enemy in the stories was pompous authority of any kind. Schoolteachers, petty officials, overbearing managers and bosses, military officers or Nazis, they were all the same, all fair game to be hoodwinked, out-schemed and defeated.

———

Once you can read, thought James, *you can do anything.*

Gran Eleanor Creighton in the front garden of number 7, Canadian Terrace

Fore Street, Port Isaac

15

Chapman's

THE GROCER'S SHOP was located on the left hand side of Fore
Street, not a lot more than a hop and a skip down from Little
Hill over the way. It occupied the ground floor of a three-storey
building, an uncommon construction height for Port Isaac, and
did what it could to provide some light relief at the base of an
otherwise stern façade. Two great windows of plate glass, so thick
that the glass had assumed an apple-green tint, filtered light on to
activities, when there were any, within the grocer's shop.

Jutting out from the three-storey building at the level of the
floor above the shop was a sign bearing the legend "L. Chapman
& Sons". The letters on the sign ran in a vertical sequence from
the top to the bottom, challenging those who could read letters
to decipher the words. The grocer's shop was, not inconsequen-
tially, known as "Chapman's".

The L. Chapman celebrated on the sign was a grocer who came
from the town of Wadebridge, a journey of a day's planning and
nine miles by either Prout's bus or the more austere National bus
out of Port Isaac. L. Chapman was clearly a courageous grocer,
quite bold enough to have established a branch of his grocery
empire in the wild outpost of Port Isaac. The "Sons" connected
with L. Chapman were unknown quantities about whom all that
was certain was that there had to be at least two of them kicking
around somewhere.

Chapman's was well placed for the convenience of the habitual
gossipmongers for whom Little Hill was the essential haven to

moor up in for a while prior to their daily round of the Fore Street Shops.

     ———

As often as not on Little Hill the greatly revered Mr Andy Oaten sat like a lord in his preferred place on one of the public benches, regaling an audience with yarns spun taller than the mighty Lobber cliff on the other side of the harbour.

Andy wore a tilted black cap with a glossy peak sticking out of it over his lively eyes. His jaw was as square as a tin of biscuits, and jutted out just far enough for a gull to build a nest on. Andy shaved, although certainly not on a daily basis. He favoured a light-coloured fisherman's smock as his general covering garment. The smock was, like Andy, worn to fragility by time, but still serviceable.

Following the conclusion of one of Andy's convoluted tales it was not unusual for one member or other of his attentive audience to declare, "Andy, that just can't be true!" Andy's reply came, "Well then missis, if ted'n true, 'tis false!"

     ———

Little Hill was contained on its upper limit by the lower wall of the primary school playground, against which the goals scored with a worn tennis ball must have been numbered in very many thousands, and the front of the Old Lifeboat House, adjacent to the school gate. The Old Lifeboat House, once the home of the Port Isaac lifeboat, was a long hollow building full of chill and echoes, fronted by massive rolling doors of battered metal painted in a weary looking dull scarlet. Whenever the doors of the Old Lifeboat House were opened and closed, the rollers never failed to screech in protest against grease rationing.

The association of the Old Lifeboat House with a lifeboat was long past. The brave men who crewed the vessel in its glory days, and defied logic by hauling the lifeboat down and up the narrow defile and tight bends of Fore Street at the respective start and end of each callout, were all "Up to St Endellion pushing up daisies", as Andy Oaten so succinctly put it.

The Old Lifeboat House had come to be leased by Chapman's, who used it to store certain of the range of goods they sold out of the nearby shop. The volume of such goods as were stored in the Old Lifeboat House was dwarfed by the vastness of the interior surroundings, although the odour of spilt paraffin from a tank on the left hand side managed to comprehensively permeate the whole extent, up, down and sideways, without any trouble at all.

———

No doubt Chapman's would have preferred a more direct view of Little Hill through the plate glass windows of the grocer's shop to the less prepossessing view that was opened in that direction, dominated as it was by the public lavatory.

The public lavatory adjoined Little Hill on its lower side. Ladies used the upper section of this building while Gentlemen diverted to the lower. The back of the public lavatory was built on the very edge of the harbour cliff. Only an insubstantial shit-house wall separated a seated spend-a-penny user of the facility, trousers around bony ankles and "enjoying a comfortable one", as Mr Jess Steer – long-term campaigner for a new public lavatory to be built in a safer location – described it, from a sudden plunge of fifty or sixty feet down to the beach below.

For all that, the public lavatory, decorated in a creamy-puce distemper set off with a green paint trim, was a presentable enough construction. The Gentlemen's section, a popular Fore Street stopping-off point for descending regulars of the Golden Lion pub, boasted standing room for four and seats for three simultaneously, and that was not counting some space for those waiting their turn. Its internal atmosphere was characterised by a noisome contest between disinfectant and stale urine, in which the latter was the clear winner on points.

The gentlemen (for, irrespective of what they were beforehand, such they became when they entered the public lavatory) clattered their customary hobnailed way from the smoky billiard room of the Liberal Club at the top of Fore Street down to the spit and sawdust public bar of the Golden Lion close to the

159

bottom. From Chapman's the gentlemen could be and assuredly would be observed as they diverted sharply to the right, united in a desire to be relieved.

—

Messrs Les Honey and Jack McOwen were numbered among the cited gentlemen. They marched purposefully down Fore Street, side by side. Les and Jack were uniformly clad in black trousers and jackets, flat caps on a modest slant, boots clacking in rhythm, perfectly in step, moving as one man.

Without breaking stride or pausing in conversation for even a second while slotting fags between their respective lips with practised hands, they curved their route in a smooth sweep towards the door of the Gentlemen's lavatory.

As if on cue, the left hands of Les and Jack reached simultaneously for their flies (their personal flies and not each other's that is to say) to commence the unbuttoning procedure, and then the two were through the public lavatory door with a style that was not far short of a triumphant flourish.

Les and Jack exhibited a deportment that might well have been choreographed in advance. Grace under pressure was manifest in their every movement. It was poetry in motion as viewed through Chapman's plate glass windows. Those who were privileged to see it were no doubt happy in the knowledge that inside the public lavatory Les and Jack pissed in all probability in precisely geometric arcs, flicked away the twin ultimate drops of pee in concert, and buttoned up their own flies again with an economy of movement as crisp as a lettuce leaf.

—

Inside Chapman's a pair of long, white marble-topped counters lined either side of a widish central area, within which customers were at liberty to move around. The counter on the left hand side was devoted to the sale of perishable goods, such as cheese, butter, margarine and lard, and was attended to by three shop assistants. Over the right hand counter, attended to by two more

160

shop assistants, the non-perishable goods, some of them tinned and others dried, were sold.

As to what lay under the counter, that was a matter for intense speculation on the part of all but the few who really knew.

A shiny, red-trimmed bacon slicer with a keen looking circular blade, manually driven, stood hopefully in the centre of the left hand counter, ready to test its edge on the occasions when there was bacon to cut. Chapman's customers looked at the bacon slicer, then looked at each other and said "If we had some bacon, we could make some bacon and eggs – if we had some eggs".

———

Yes, Chapman's also had no bananas.

———

Chapman's sometimes did stock eggs for sale, some of them with the kind of inherent freshness that a curate might have admired. In the absence of real eggs, blue-paper wrapped packages of a yellowish powder known as "dried eggs" were always an option and could be used to prepare a not unacceptable scrambled egg dish. Gulls' eggs were a better alternative to dried eggs in season, and moorhens' eggs were even better still. However, Chapman's did not sell any of those.

Ranked up close to the bacon slicer were, not necessarily in order of precedence, an enormous thick-rinded cheese, and great blocks of butter and margarine, from all of which tiny portions, exactly equivalent to the quantity prescribed as the standard ration, were dug out and meticulously weighed for customers who were able to present a valid ration book.

In front of the right hand counter a row of open tins of biscuits leered at prospective customers. There were "Cream Crackers", "Marie", "Nice", "Rich Tea" and "Digestive" varieties to name a few, and a few is more or less what they were. The biscuits were sold by the pound in largish brown paper bags of the kind that made such a satisfying explosion when they were blown full of air and burst with a clap of the hands directly behind an unsuspecting victim.

Broken biscuits cost less than their unbroken counterparts. It was therefore prudent for customers to retrieve their own measure of biscuits from the open tins and to break as many biscuits as possible while doing so. Dipping half a biscuit in a cup of tea was just as satisfying an action as dipping a whole biscuit. Half a biscuit soaked up the tea more efficiently than a whole one in any case. The trouble with dipping a whole biscuit in tea was that a fair bit of the biscuit often dropped off into the tea and sank down to lose itself in the tea leaves at the bottom of the cup.

———

Mr Jack Provis was an imposing presence behind Chapman's left hand counter. Jack stood tall and sleek in a white dustcoat. The gloss on Jack's hair rivalled the gleam on the static disc blade of the bacon slicer.

Jack was an ex-serviceman and an accomplished pianist whose great musical gift was the toast of many wartime NAAFI establishments. In the Port Isaac Civvy Street that he returned to after demobilisation, Jack extended his talents as the masterful organist at St Peter's Church, where he played the organ regularly at services for many years. It was worth going to St Peter's just to hear Jack's voluntary renditions of "Jesu, joy of man's desiring" and "I know that my Redeemer liveth".

Jack's great tour de force on the organ was probably the "Trumpet Voluntary". This classic number was probably never played anywhere more heart-stirringly, or more triumphantly, or with more raise-the-church-roof power than it was by Jack Provis when Jack was in his prime.

———

The manager of Chapman's was a gentleman named Mr Hillman, by his own admission nothing more or less than an unabashed extrovert. Mr Hillman lived in a bungalow in the flat part of lower Trewetha Lane, not far up beyond the Temperance Hall. If Mr Hillman had a Christian name, no one gave any impression of having heard what it was.

Mr Hillman was an exceedingly dapper figure in a craftily cut suit, or alternatively in a dark blazer and grey flannels. His movements were as precise as they were graceful. On Mr Hillman's Brylcreem-enriched hair the comb strokes were like fixed plough lines crossing a well trimmed lawn.

Mr Hillman had an intrusive manner of speaking using a mildly off-cockney accent that tended to get under a listener's fingernails after a while. It was the type of accent that could, in a more sophisticated part of the country, have typed Mr Hillman as a cross coming somewhere between Mr Arthur English's "Prince of the Wide Boys" and Mr Charles Dickens' Uriah Heep.

Irrespective of any tendency he had to unctuousness, Mr Hillman was a dynamic organiser with an indefatigable community spirit. He frequently appeared, and always excelled, as Master of Ceremonies at talent contests and charity concerts in both the Temperance Hall and the Church Rooms. All of his routines as compère were small masterpieces of the man rising above the quality of his material.

Mr Hillman's signature performance was to divide the invariably capacity concert audiences into two distinct groups, one group occupying one half of the hall and the other group occupying the other half. Any parallel of this separation with the aisle-divided layout of Chapman's may have been no accident. One group would be charged with singing "It's a long way to Tipperary" (or, as Teddy Bush always characterised the song, "It's the wrong way to tickle Mary"), while at the same time their opposite numbers in the other group were ordered to sing, "Pack up your troubles in your old kit bag".

The winning group was the one that drowned out the other with the power of its choral might. This mass exercise of combat-by-song generally made for better audience entertainment than did the on-stage talent, about which the kindest thing to be declared was that it was a fortunate thing that misrepresentation was not a crime.

"Grandma's Chair", near Port Gaverne

16

Wreck

FLOTSAM AND JETSAM were a celebrated performing double act. To piano accompaniment they specialised in gentle comic songs, some of which may well have been funny, although James wasn't too sure about that. He had heard Flotsam and Jetsam a few times on the wireless, both in *Workers' Playtime*, which always came from a canteen located somewhere or other, and also on the Saturday favourite *Henry Hall's Guest Night*, which had no connection with a canteen at all.

The soft voiced Mr Henry Hall, one of the big boys said to James at school, had two brothers, respectively named Ass Hall and Bugger Hall. *Bugger Hall's Guest Night might have been a good programme to listen to,* James thought.

Flotsam and Jetsam were perhaps not bad performers, but in terms of double acts that sang songs, James much preferred Kenneth and George, who called themselves The Western Brothers. Kenneth and George were not only very funny when drawling out their songs on the wireless about playing the game chaps and wearing the old school tie, but their adventures could also be followed in the comic *Radio Fun*.

To give Flotsam and Jetsam their due, their particular names were something of an education for those who knew what the names meant and what the difference was between them. In the manner of stalactites and stalagmites, flotsam and jetsam were separate parts of a single process. All that really had to be known was which part of the process was which.

Most of the boys were never able to work out whether the stalactite part was the bit on the roof or the piece on the floor – that is until one of the teachers told them that stalactites held tight to the roof and stalagmites lay mighty on the floor. One of the boys asked, did a stalactite become a stalagmite if it fell off the roof onto the floor? The teacher didn't know.

It was easier to distinguish flotsam from jetsam. Flotsam floated in the sea and jetsam didn't, at least until it was thrown back in.

The term "flotsam" more or less accounted for anything that could float until it became waterlogged and sank. Its derivation could be either animal, or vegetable or mineral. The range of possibilities stopped only just short of the abstract that they liked to invoke on *Twenty Questions* on the wireless, in which programme Jack Train, an almost-Cornishman from Plymouth, provided the corny banter.

Perhaps most importantly, although this was not part of any official definition, flotsam offered the ever-present potential to become jetsam and be retrieved by a finder.

Jetsam was therefore bolstered by the great hope that sprang so eternal in any beachcomber's or cliff ranger's breast when those worthies sought out the fruits of the sea stranded on the shingle or caught up in the rocks when the tide went out, ready and waiting to be possessed by whoever got to them first.

"What's the difference between flotsam and jetsam?" was a stock question that was regularly passed around the school playground, although the time eventually came when everyone knew the answer and no one could be caught out by it any more.

Fortunately this once valiant attempt to trap the uninformed never came to replace the most beloved of playground standard riddles, "When is a door not a door?"

166

Answer: "When it is ajar!"
Response of questioner: "Then piss in it and drink my health!"

———

Equally redolent of the exchanges of those happy days was, "He's looking for you!"
"Who is looking for me?"
"Chunky!"
"Who is Chunky?
"He's a man with pineapple balls!"

———

Sooner or later everyone in the playground, except maybe the girls, caught on to that undying tribute to tinned fruit as well.

———

The incidental answer to the difference between flotsam and jetsam was that there was no difference between the two at all. As far as the Port Isaac boys were concerned both commodities were classed as "wreck".

The critical judgement behind defining any material carried and delivered by the sea as wreck was not so much that the material should have any inherent value but rather that it should be capable of being useful to its finder. There were few pieces of wreck that could not be put to some good use, somehow or other.

It was the finder's task to bridge the common linkage between flotsam and jetsam as wreck. If a good-looking piece of wreck spotted adrift offshore showed a reluctance to move onshore and become jetsam, there were more than a few of the boys who were prepared to go into the sea after it and drag it into compliance, thereby turning the tables at a stroke.

———

Wreck arrived along the coast of Port Isaac Bay on the furrowed brow of storms. Even before a storm waned and subsided, the boys took to the beaches and the cliffs in search of wreck, and there they found it: odd bits of wood, rough, barnacle burrowed baulks of timber, planks, pit props, lumps of cork and sometimes even a fragment of a ship's superstructure. Generally when they thought about wreck the boys thought of it in terms of wood.

Wave-tossed pieces of wood, rolled by the sea and honed by contact with the rocks, had usually lost any pretensions to plane edges or regular shape by the time the boys found them. However, all such wreck made good firewood when it dried out, and that was just about as useful as it could ever be.

Wreck's greatest prize was one of the big green glass ball floats that the deep-sea fishermen used to support their nets. Although rough seas, a rocky coast and thin glass didn't make a promising equation, some glass balls found their intact way through – by guess and by God it was surmised.

———

As finders of wreck, the Port Isaac boys knew that they were, as often as not, benefiting from the misfortune, the loss, or possibly a tragic end suffered by those in peril on the sea. It would be fitting to believe that this thought weighed greatly on the boys' minds, but in truth it didn't count for anything at all. Wreck was believed to be as much a part of the harvest of the sea, there for the taking by those who dared to go after it, as was any fish, crab or lobster brought up from the deep, or winkle gathered into a bucket on the edge of the harbour, or lugworm dug from the sand of the beach beneath its tell-tale casts.

———

In association with pieces of wreck, storms also transported great spreading rafts of tangled strands of oar weed, and threw high mounds of torn kelp and a host of other seaweed types, laced through with cuttlefish bones and mermaids purses, up on the foreshore.

The banked up seaweed was collected by eager gardeners, shovelled into wheelbarrows and rolled away to enrich their soil. When the quantity of seaweed was large, it was common to see a farmer down on the beach, pitch-forking seaweed into a cart while his horse stood by looking equally as aloof as an up country visitor taking in the view.

———

It was the historical tradition of acquiring bounty by deliberately luring ships onto the rocks around the coast of Cornwall, through the strategic placement of onshore lights, that defined the process popularly referred to as "wrecking". The process probably owed more to myth than to reality. However, it worked well enough as a basis for some good yarns.

———

The code of conduct for anyone who collected a piece of wreck on a beach required that the piece be carried to a location well above the high-tide mark. There the piece could be left for as long as the finder wanted to leave it, a time generally determined by how much time the piece took to dry out, as to one degree or another freshly recovered wreck was always rather waterlogged.

Above the high-water mark, a piece of wreck was held to be sacrosanct. No one other than the finder would touch it. It lay in the open in total security that was observed by all – well, nearly all anyway.

———

There was a vague understanding by the boys that the retrieving of any wreck had, by law, to be reported to the coastguards, but if anyone had ever made such a report in practice with reference to the nondescript pieces of worn wreck that were the norm, it was never obvious. Usually in practice both parties, coastguards and finders, turned a blind eye in one another's direction.

Port Isaac could lay claim to a firm contingent, three in number, of HM Coastguard. The coastguard station was a terrace of dwellings in behind the Rivoli cinema, commanding a clear view of Port Isaac Bay, and exposed to every extreme of weather that the Atlantic could throw at it.

The members of the coastguard contingent had several qualities in common. They were of Welsh nationality, their wives were sharp tongued (no surprise there), and having an easy time was their goal in life. Or so it was alleged.

———

One day when carrying a length of wreck in the direction of his home, James, a regular on the wrecking path, was stopped by a Port Isaac coastguard, who asked James where he had just come from. James told the official that he had been wrecking down along the cliffs. The coastguard told James he was going to pretend he hadn't heard him say that.

The coastguard went on to tell James, in quite strong terms, that all wreck, flotsam or jetsam, it didn't much matter, was the property of a gentleman who bore the grand title of "Receiver of Wreck", for whom he, as a member of HM Coastguard, was a representative. The coastguard made the Receiver of Wreck appear as if he were a god to whom the coastguards were acolytes serving as angels.

The Receiver of Wreck sounded to James to be some behind-the-scenes threat designed to assure a fearful respect for the kind of authority for which neither much fear nor respect existed in the first place.

———

James could only wonder as he was sent on his way by the coastguard, surprisingly enough for once without even a clip around the ear to encourage him, just what the dreaded Receiver of Wreck would do with the old piece of firewood-destined wreck that James was carrying. The Receiver of Wreck might also have his work cut out to decide what to do with the odd array of other lengths of drying wreck lying on the grass that James had recently passed out at Pine Awn.

On the other hand James had no doubt that the Receiver of Wreck would, in the person of his coastguard representative, certainly have coveted a green glass ball if James had had one of those.

The transport garages (Prout Bros., North Cornwall Transport and Central) flanking New Road, looking in the direction of the top of Back Hill

The view from William John's salon

17

William John

IT WAS IN A FORMER single room cottage that the Port Isaac gentlemen's barber, Mr William John Honey, maintained his barber's salon. The single room was located on the other side of a curtain-draped opening to the right of a hallway. No doubt some kind of door had once occupied the opening before it was removed, maybe for chopping up as firewood.

That William John's establishment catered for the tonsorial needs of gentlemen was a recognized fact. That a large number of William John's customers were to gentlemen just about what gull shit was to a line of clean washing was yet another fact. William John's customers of course also included boys, some of who might in the course of time aspire to become gentlemen, although there were few Port Isaac men who would have taken a bet on that ever happening.

The barber's shop was located on the harbour side of Fore Street. A bay window at the back looked out over the harbour and framed a panoramic view of all of Roscarrock Hill and a bit of Lobber field. The front entry on Fore Street was no more than ten paces downhill from that other celebrated gentlemen's precinct in the public lavatory, or forty paces downhill from the billiard room of the Liberal Club, or perhaps twenty paces uphill from the ultimate inner sanctum for both gentlemen and near gentlemen, namely the public bar of the Golden Lion.

In the course of a short stroll down Fore Street, an aspiring gentleman on the loose with a few bob in his pocket would, given the range of the said facilities offered to him, be able to enjoy a game of billiards or a shit or a shave or a haircut or a pint of flat beer, or all of them in sequence. He could smoke a fag or two in the process and not have to return home until Harry Irons, the landlord of the Golden Lion yelled, in richly accented Welsh tones, "Time gentlemen, please!" to his habitués, and in some cases to the sons of his habitués. Taken altogether, the prospect was not only pleasing but also difficult to improve on.

William John's barber's shop was unable to boast of modern conveniences, but such conveniences as existed were fit for the purpose, so there it was.

The speciality haircut of the establishment was a "short back and sides and some off the top". It was possible for a customer to request any other style of haircutting as well, and William John was always ready to oblige, as long as the customer understood that what he got would probably look not unlike a short back and sides and some off the top.

The main feature of William John's barber's shop was a barber's chair of considerable antiquity. The chair was fitted with a fearsome looking brass bound mechanism evidently designed to permit it not only to swivel but also to recline and elevate, although not with all actions necessarily taking place at the same time. It was not that it mattered much as the mechanism was jammed up and hadn't worked since William John acquired the chair.

To raise the heads of Port Isaac boys to a convenient level at which William John could mount an attack on their heads that might or might not include a carefully placed pudding basin to trim around, a wooden plank was laid across the arms of the chair for the boys to sit on. The professional service that they received from William John was incomparable. No appointments were necessary, the nearest frills were keeping a respectful distance, and the price the boys paid per haircut was only sixpence.

——

A large mirror within an ornate rim was mounted on the wall that the barber's chair faced. The mirror was fastened to the wall so securely that it might have been an original feature of the room, a tight companion to the wall long before the barber's chair was dragged in to confront it.

The mirror appeared to be gradually succumbing to an insidious form of creeping disease. Brownish tendrils reached into the silvered glass from the rim of the mirror, and were, in the opinion of regular customers, obviously gaining ground. The corners of the mirror were coming appreciably close to being blotted out by evil grey clouds of seeping infection.

In the mirror, a customer seated either on the chair, or on the plank across its arms with a near-white sheet around his neck and William John circling him like a sparrow hawk in pursuit of the barber's art, was able to gaze on a reflection of the salon as seen through a glass, darkly. There was an alcove at the back on the right in which supplies of barber's trade staples were kept, including large bottles of Bay Rum and the deadly dangerous sounding styptic pencils. When the active end of a styptic pencil was applied by William John to treat an occasional shaving wound, it not only staunched any flow of blood but also induced the wounded patron to leap from the barber's chair with a bloodcurdling scream.

——

In the centre of the wall at the back, directly behind the barber's chair, was a stone cold fireplace from which no cheery fire was permitted to cast a comforting glow. The fireplace found a much better function as an ideal repository for dead matches and spit-soaked fag ends.

Any call for warmth was only associated with the winter months in any case, and was then provided by a paraffin heater.

Those who doubted that the heater was fed with paraffin had only to sniff the surrounding atmosphere for all questions to be removed.

———

The internal décor of the barber's shop was completed by a row of hard seated wooden chairs lined up along the Fore Street wall on the left of the barber's chair. On these chairs William John's customers waited for their turn to have a haircut come along.

———

Directly below the mirror there was a china sink, vitreous and manufactured by Messrs Shanks, according to an inscription on its surface. When plugged, the sink was used by William John not only for mixing shaving foam but also for the occasional washing of a customer's hair that he might be requested to do. Hair washing in a public place, or even in a private place as far as that went, was an event so rare that when it came to pass people felt motivated to come along to witness it. Removing the long-term accumulated residue of repeated applications of Brylcreem and not a little adhering foreign matter from hair, let alone the odd flea, was a sure bet to test the limits of the most potent soap to be obtained.

The vitreous china sink was just a sink, no more and no less than that. It had no connection with running water. Its outlet was fitted with a length of rubber hose leading down to a bucket. Shaving and hair-washing water had its particular fount in a second bucket, heated over a primus.

———

William John lived in one of the aptly named "Old" council houses, in a fortress-like terrace of the same standing on Trewetha Lane just above its junction with New Road on the outskirts of Port Isaac. He had fought hard through the war and survived, in all his modesty, not to tell the tale. William John was a returned hero. Never appearing to be in a hurry, because he almost certainly never was, this most self-effacing of men performed his barber's duties promptly, with a gentle ease of manner and a full measure of kind words to his customers.

William John was limited in stature but huge in spirit. He had a long forehead, suggestive of great wisdom, from which his hair rippled backwards in a set of undulating waves. No one knew where William John got his own haircut.

———

The barber's trade tools employed by William John were fundamental, consisting of a pair of scissors, a comb and a set of hand-activated hair clippers. He shaved his patrons with one or other of a pair of deadly looking cutthroat razors that he stropped to keenness with a perfectly rhythmic beat on a thick leather strap attached by one of its ends to a nail in the wall to the right of the mirror.

On the day that William John took delivery of his first pair of electrically powered hair clippers he was besieged by customers eager to see and experience being ministered to by this new technological miracle. As it was, William John's mastery of this new technological miracle was not achieved overnight. "Is it pulling?" he asked as the electric clippers summarily ripped clumps of hair from the back of a customer's neck.

As an accessory to the electric clippers, William John then obtained a Bakelite disc studded with a close-set spiral of short blunt tines. This implement was slotted into the clippers and applied to the head for the purpose of scalp massage. A muted hum emanated from the clippers as the disc vibrated wildly against a customer's scalp and induced the lucky customer's eyes to lose focus. The cost of this service was three pence on top of the haircut price. The service was reckoned by those who experienced it to be worth all of that, and more.

———

If on most evenings William John's salon was full of potential customers, on Saturday evenings it was full to overflowing. Some of those who came in on Saturday evenings might even have arrived with the intention of having a haircut or a shave.

For most of the Saturday evening crowd, the attraction at William John's was the type of chitchat and banter that took place in a closed male preserve. It was men only that were supposed to be in at that time, but if boys were careful and crept quietly into corners or lay mute under the row of chairs, their presence was suffered. They heard much in the way of new words and the conduct of unusual practices, some of which they understood, and some of which they didn't.

—

William John stood centre stage as the master of ceremonies. He moderated the discussions with a dry and easy charm while snipping, clipping and sweeping fallen hair into a greasy, grey and black, ever-growing pile on the cracked linoleum floor.

The Terrace and, parked on the right, one of the Prout Brothers' buses

Port Isaac harbour at low tide

18

About Ice Cream

THE WHEELHOUSE was located on the right hand side of the Town Platt, the right hand side, that is, of anyone standing on the Town Platt and facing towards the harbour. If that same person turned around to look back along Middle Street, and frankly, the view of the harbour was to be preferred, then the Wheelhouse would be over on his left hand side.

The Wheelhouse was the property of Mr and Mrs Tommy Atkins. Although "Tommy" might have been a rather unoriginal nickname accorded to Mr Atkins, it was probable that Tommy was a genuine Christian name, no doubt derived from familiar considerations of Thomas.

Tommy Atkins was a short man, with slightly hunched shoulders. His complexion was sallow, and his hair was dark. He was never seen without a fag dangling precariously from his rather full lips. From his general appearance he would not have been out of place at all on a First World War battlefield, and that made his name even more credible and appropriate.

Tommy met his end under tragic circumstances not entirely disconnected from the more recent war and its aftermath. He did duty as a part-time coast watcher, which meant that he was required for a directed period of either day or night to be assigned to one or other of four coast watcher huts established at suitable vantage points along Port Isaac Bay between Port Quin and Tregardock.

The four huts were respectively sited, from west to east, at Kellan Head near Port Quin; adjacent to the cliff path about half way along between Port Isaac and Port Gaverne; in the vicinity of Bounds Cliff half a mile up from Port Gaverne; and on the cliff top above the old slate quarry at Donkey's Hole a couple of miles above Port Gaverne. The Donkey's Hole hut was established on land belonging to Tregardock farm and was popularly referred to as "Garget".

Between them the four huts commanded the open arc of the entire Port Isaac Bay. The Bounds Cliff and Garget huts were constructed of concrete, whereas the other two were wooden prefabricated structures.

Tommy was unfortunate enough to be involved in night duties at the Kellan Head hut on a night when both the wooden construction and Tommy were consumed by fire. The more grue-some aspects of the accident were mulled over, in indulgent post mortem detail, by Fore Street regulars at Little Hill and on the Pentice for a very long time afterwards. It made vital grist for their mill.

The expression "Foul play cannot be ruled out" gained solemn currency in conversation. However, the only one who really knew what took place on that fateful night was Tommy, and he was not in a position to set the record straight.

———

Be that as it may, when Tommy was in his pre-mortem state, he and Mrs Atkins ran a café on the lower floor of the Wheelhouse, at the Town Platt level. Their café was graced with the imaginative name of the Wheelhouse Café. The Wheelhouse was equipped with two more floors above its ground floor, the upper floor of which was in under the eaves of the steeply peaked roof.

———

Mrs Tommy Atkins was a dark haired, buxom lady with the aspect of a forcibly retired belly dancer. She gained a short period of fame with the Port Isaac boys when she introduced into the bill

182

of fare of the Wheelhouse Café a product that Tibby Thomas described as "water ice cream".

In a prevailing climate of restricted ice cream production and uncertain delivery to Port Isaac of such ice cream as there was to be delivered, there was an obvious niche to be filled, and Mrs Tommy Atkins was just the one who moved to fill it. The Wheelhouse Café was equipped with a refrigerator, which meant that at least one key prerequisite was taken care of.

The water ice cream was coloured red. It was prepared by virtue of adding some form of supplement to tap water and freezing the ensuing solution. The product was sold in grainy, rectangular, icy chunks shoved straight into the customer's hand.

Whatever supplement went into the water ice cream had a taste that would have taken a markedly sensitive tongue to detect. The flavour was as elusive as the Scarlet Pimpernel and was as rarely discovered. It was possible for the customer to suck out the coloured component and be left with an equally tasteless handful of dripping ice.

When the novelty value of the water ice cream had worn off, there was found to be not enough sustaining grace left in its substance to keep the product alive.

Mrs Cecil Brimacombe, celebrated actress of the Temperance Hall stage and offbeat drummer with the "Rivolians" trio, provided the final coup de grace to the ailing water ice cream. For an enterprising period of time Mrs Brimmy ran a small greengrocery establishment in an annex to the Liberal Club in Fore Street at the foot of Back Hill.

Mrs Brimmy progressed along and beyond the water ice cream route by freezing a range of mixtures of juice, pop, water and honey in eggcups with small flat wooden sticks frozen into the mixture to make for ease of handling.

The demand for Mrs Brimmy's prototype ice lollipops overwhelmed the rate at which they could be produced. Her sales of ice lollipops eclipsed those of her greengrocery by a long, long margin. When she gave up the shop, on grounds of age and fading health, it was a time for genuine lamentation by her host of dedicated customers.

The inspired title of water ice cream handed by Tibby Thomas to Mrs Tommy Atkins' subsequently eclipsed product distinguished that product from two other varieties of more conventional ice cream that were occasionally available in Port Isaac. One of these was a variety home made by Mr Jim May, sold in Jim's greengrocery shop in Victoria House across from Rowe's, the newsagents, in lower Fore Street. The other variety of ice cream was a commercial product made by J. Lyons and named "Lyons Maid". Lyons Maid was in the purvey of Mrs Lynwood Cowling at her Old Drug Store, a combined chemist and bric-a-brac shop located at the bottom of Back Hill on the upper corner that it made with Fore Street.

The Old Drug Store was familiarly referred to as "the chemist's", or more simply still as "Mrs Cowling's", in a tribute to the dynamic lady of the establishment, about whom any allegations of loudness or outrageousness of character would have easily stood up to cross-examination in a court of law.

A sign in Old English script over the lower entry to Mrs Cowling's purported to announce to those who could read that here indeed was "The Old Drug Store". However, the nature of the Old English script – or perhaps it was the nature of the old English sign writer – was such that the sign always appeared to read as "The Old Drug Score".

Mrs Cowling's powerful personality turned her into a significantly larger than life figure. In public she appeared overdressed, over-painted and not infrequently overbearing. She was subject to extreme swings of mood that could manifest themselves, all within the space of a hour, as much in acts of unlimited generosity to her customers as in rudeness and miserliness of spirit directed at the selfsame people.

Mrs Cowling lived above the Old Drug Store in company with her husband Lynwood and an exceedingly unpleasant and highly pampered Pekinese dog named Billy. Billy enjoyed the bulk of Mrs Cowling's attention, although it was Lynwood who was almost certainly better trained than Billy.

———

Lynwood was a most agreeable man. He was balding, with a perpetually harried expression on his face and an almost inevitable resident fag in his mouth. He moved with such alacrity at Mrs Cowling's behest that he became popularly known as "Lightning Lyn".

Lynwood, who was responsible for the maintenance of the stock in the shop, never appeared behind the shop counter unless he either was in hurried transit or had arrived there by accident. Mrs Cowling fronted the operation of the shop.

———

Mrs Cowling's shop was divided into two sections. There was a lower section on the corner of Back Hill where pharmaceutical items and patent remedies were on sale, and an upper section, reached either by climbing two steps up from the lower or through its own door further up Fore Street. In the upper section such items as sweets, cigarettes, souvenirs, mementoes, postcards, buckets and spades, shrimping nets and beach balls were available.

There were even a few books to be seen on display. Mrs Cowling, much to the benefit of the boys, stocked the excellent "Observer's" series of little hard-covered guidebooks covering, among other subjects, *British Birds*, *Birds' Eggs* (invaluable that one), *Trees*, *Insects*, *Wildflowers*, *Butterflies*, *Grasses, Sedges and Rushes* and *Animals*.

Both sections of Mrs Cowling's were imbued with a sweet, piny, medicinal smell, diffusing in the first instance from the pharmaceutical section, and all overlain, not to say overpowered, by the stronger odour sifting away from Mrs Cowling's thick mask of face powder and liberal application of perfume.

———

Billy the peke lay on a fluffy cushion outside the entry to the pharmaceutical section and glared malevolently at all passers by, most of whom gave him a very wide berth. It was wiser for customers to enter Mrs Cowling's via the door to the upper section in order to avoid having Billy take a surreptitious nip at their ankles.

Fortunately for many customers, Billy was evidently not subject to the same rationing regime as they were. Billy was so grossly overfed and was consequently of such corpulence that his ability to make a sudden move was not nearly as effective as that of Lynwood. The only occasions on which Billy moved with great despatch was when he was motivated to do so by the toe of a customer who had finally had enough.

Since even to look askance at Billy ensured that a customer would incur the everlasting displeasure of Mrs Cowling, a well-placed kick up Billy's backside by a customer could be absolutely guaranteed to cut off a nose to spite a face. Mrs Cowling had ultimate power over the weekly two-ounce sweet ration for those customers who chose to get their quota from her, and if she was caught on a good day, she could often be rather flexible with her scales for those whom she favoured. The exact converse applied to customers who were in Mrs Cowling's bad books.

———

If the news was about that Mrs Cowling was in a good mood, then ration books were at once carried to her for clipping in the likely expectation that a few extra boiled sweets would end up in the paper bag. A day did not get much better than that.

Mrs Cowling's sweets were displayed in a row of large, wide

mouthed glass jars. Fruit drops stood alongside liquorice allsorts, red and white striped mints vied for attention with toffees, gob-stoppers loomed over aniseed balls, and a few sticks of rock leaned over the rare bars of chocolate. They offered a feast for the eyes, but only two official ounces per week for the mouth.

———

The welcome advent of Lyons Maid ice cream at Mrs Cowling's however, did much to extend the limitations of the sweet ration. Lyons Maid was delivered to Mrs Cowling packed in dry ice in a red, lead-lined crate marked with the name of J. Lyons, the manufacturer. The delivery was irregular, but all that was delivered was sold out in almost the blink of an eye. A queue formed up prior to an announcement of the anticipated arrival of a consignment.

What a customer got with Lyons Maid was a little cylinder of ice cream, marginally wider than it was high, encased around its outside perimeter in yellow paper that was peeled away with eagerness to get at the contents. The travelling association of the ice cream with dry ice rendered the ice cream hard and rigid. The boys liked to draw their teeth across the ice cream, ploughing shallow grooves. The drawn out slivers of ice cream filled their mouths with ecstasy as they burst into melting flavour.

When the Lyons Maid ice cream was sold out, Mrs Cowling discarded the dry ice into Fore Street as having served its purpose. The boys vied with each other to get hold of chunks of dry ice, tossing them from hand to hand to prevent cold burns, not always successfully. Placed in water, the dry ice bubbled furiously and generated pools of mysterious white mist.

———

Jim May's version of ice cream became so soaringly popular, that in Miss Smythe's infants' class at the school, a new verse was added to the song "Do you know the Muffin Man?" and was sung by the class with infinitely more gusto than were the original words from which the verse was derived.

We call him Jim, the ice cream man,
We call him Jim, the ice cream man,
We call him Jim, the ice cream man,
He lives down Ice Cream Lane!

Long-term fame was not to attend Jim's ice cream endeavours, however, as either Jim's ice cream may have been less hygienically prepared than it ought to have been or perhaps his refrigerating facilities may have been less efficient than might have been thought desirable.

When more than a few of the young consumers who had hitherto so cheerfully sung Jim's praises began breaking out into rashes allegedly attributable to Jim's ice cream, Jim's trade, great while it lasted, suffered an overnight demise.

———

It was a demise that was as complete as that of the Wheelhouse Café's water ice cream under the assault of Mrs Brimmy's ice lollipops, and that of the late and much lamented Tommy Atkins.

A fishing boat slipping between the breakwaters on a rising tide

Port Gaverne harbour

19

Ted

THE HARBOUR CAFÉ, on the corner made by Fore Street with Middle Street at the back of the Town Platt, was owned and run by Mr Ted Robinson and his wife Ruth.

Both Ted and Ruth were commendable artists. Ruth was a daughter of the celebrated artist of the "Newlyn School", Mr Douglas Pinder, and specialised in serious Cornish landscape studies, painting under her maiden name. Ted, a Lancastrian in exile who had, entirely to his own satisfaction, graduated from the ranks of foreigners to attain the title of honorary Cornishman, was accomplished in preparing pen and ink sketches of local scenes, of which he maintained an excellent portfolio.

Ted additionally had a natural talent for drawing cartoons and caricatures and for illustrating comic verses, some of which he claimed to have written himself, and for all anyone else knew, probably had.

The problem with Ted of course was that it was never altogether possible for anyone to confidently believe everything (or even anything) that Ted told him.

The little building that housed the Harbour Café was reputed to be several centuries old. A weathered Bakelite plaque on its front wall facing towards the Town Platt said as much. The inscription on the plaque went on to advise that the Harbour Café had had a featured role in such long forgotten epics of the cinema as

Phantom Light, starring Gordon Harker, and *Sea Mist*, starring no one, as *Sea Mist* was a documentary film.

It was Gordon Harker's illustrious association with the lower part of Port Isaac that caused Gordon Keat, whose mother ran the fish and chip shop a couple of doors up along the gully of Fore Street from the Harbour Café, to be nicknamed "Arker".

———

Harbour Café, under Ted and Ruth's proprietorship, found further fame as a centre for light refreshments and the purchase of souvenirs, some elements of either of which were known to be more desirable than others.

The souvenir trade out of the Harbour Cafe had a basis in Ted and Ruth's artistic output, as well as in a variety of blown glass animals (all of which contrived to look like contorted dachshund dogs), in a selection of Frith's or Valentine's or Salmon's postcards, in hand-painted pebbles and, in a unique speciality, in ashtrays, lamp stands and decorative knick-knacks made of lathe-turned and polished serpentine quarried at the Lizard in west Cornwall and marketed under the brand name "Lyonesse".

———

If ever a man existed who could render a donkey three legged by virtue of a capacity to spout genuine bullshit until the cows not only came home but drooped their heads in despair as well, Ted was that man. Ted was a prince of the interminable monologue. He was a born salesman. His wits were his living.

Ted was able to tell anyone prepared to listen to him what he was going to tell them, following which he would tell them, and after that he would tell them what he had told them. Ruth floated passively around the edge of Ted's rivers of words, having long ago thrown in the towel on her ability to punctuate the verbal flood with rationality.

That which lifted Ted resolutely above the rank of being a

mere local bore was the rich glow of his humour, the sharpness of his observations, and a peppery seasoning of intellect that turned his labyrinthine discourses into an art form.

He was inordinately proud of the fact that he had once, by his own admission, allegedly won an argument within the confines of the Harbour Café with none other than Mr Wilfred Pickles, one of Britain's most celebrated proponents of the practice of verbal overkill.

Wilfred was the presenter of the famous weekly wireless programme *Have a Go!* Few who owned a wireless ever missed a broadcast of Wilfred's programme. Wilfred took it to rural halls all around the nation, describing the programme's contents as "a spot of homely fun, presenting the people to the people". In the typical course of *Have a Go!* local rustics would be patronisingly interviewed and, chiefly at their own expense, be induced to sing along to the accompaniment of Miss Violet Carson at the piano, so as to generate merriment in the audience.

Wilfred's willing have-a-go victims were able to win a few shillings by answering some simple questions. If they got the answers right, and they almost always did, with as much prompting from Wilfred as was necessary to make recompense for any humiliation they had formerly suffered at his hands, the money was handed over to them by Mr Barney Colehan, the producer of *Have a Go!*. The accompanying catch phrase from Wilfred, "Give him the money, Barney!", was universally known and celebrated as an essential part of the vernacular.

Ted's defeat of Wilfred in closed debate, if it ever happened, deserved to be considered a monumental event, given Wilfred's immense stature. This duel of giants was fought many times over by Ted in one-way dialogue to anyone he could trap in a corner, although the nature of the actual exchanges between Ted and Wilfred never quite came to be clarified.

Ted was a powerfully dapper man. He was so thin that it was reputed that he would be invisible if he stood sideways. Alternatively, it was claimed that it would be safer for Ted to remain indoors on a windy day in order to avoid being blown away.

Ted's head glistened under a thick application of hair oil, the operative word being oil. He sported a clipped toothbrush moustache of the type favoured by Mr Douglas Fairbanks Junior, a swashbuckling actor to whom Ted bore some resemblance when seen in an imperfect light.

Ted drove around the lanes of north Cornwall in a low-slung beige-coloured Jaguar car. The Jaguar, like Ted, was pretty much one of a kind. It once achieved eighty miles per hour on the road up to Delabole above China Downs. It was heady stuff.

———

There were wispy rumours, never confirmed, that Ted performed a clandestine function during the war, watching the coast for signs of the enemy, identifying likely spies, keeping an ear open for the kind of careless talk which might cost lives. In spite of his personal brand of supremely careless talk Ted gave nothing of this away, either then or after. There may well have been more to Ted than the mere slickness that met the eye.

———

Ted did not see active service in a theatre of war, which naturally failed to endear him to those who did. Any men who spent the war at home or in a "safe" billet for whatever reason, fairly or unfairly, whether on grounds of medical incapacity or mental instability, or of work in a reserved occupation or conscientious objection, all carried forward into the post-war years a stigma that would not be allowed to fade away.

Those who profited from the war were especially resented by those who did not, irrespective of the amount of active service the latter may (or may not) have undertaken.

———

Ted and Ruth had an only son named Tony, a boy with a bright mind but very delicate health. Tony inherited a measure of Ted's wit. One fateful day in the school playground, when Tony was reciting a verse entitled "Bollicks Bill" (who went up the hill to have a game of cricket only to have the ball go up his trouser leg and hit his middle wicket), Raymond ("Ido") Glover was heard to address Tony as "Bollicks".

"Bollicks" was immediately installed as a nickname that stuck to Tony like the strongest of glue.

If Ted happened to be within hearing distance when any boy referred to Tony as "Bollicks", Ted was certain to fall immediately into an apoplectic rage. The recognition of the incendiary quality of Ted's reaction to the stimulus of "Hey, Bollicks!" only tended to institutionalise Tony's nickname further.

———

Boys took to passing Harbour Cottage – where Ted, Ruth, Tony and Ted's mother "Nan" lived adjacent to Chapman's across from Little Hill on Fore Street – and calling up the steep flight of slate steps for "Bollicks" to come out and play. The boys were ready to take to their heels at the very instant of Ted's thunderously irate appearance at the top of the steps.

———

One late autumn evening James was standing at the door of the public lavatory on Fore Street looking up at Harbour Cottage across the way, waiting for Warren Dinner (known as "Flynner" or "Flynn" through association of his surname with that of the great and versatile film star Mr Errol Flynn) to complete spending his penny within one of the lavatory stalls.

Flynner was a couple of years older than James. For all that James knew, Flynner might have very well been moving his bowels in the paid stall he had selected, or he might equally have been penning a short verse on the wall of the stall. In the event of his undertaking the latter activity he would not have been the first such author by a long margin.

James knew that Ted was eager to get his hands on Flynner in connection with Flynner's failure to attend a recent rehearsal for the annual pantomime at the Temperance Hall. Flynner had a leading role in the pantomime, as did Ted, who had been not inappropriately cast as the villain.

Ted appeared at the door of Harbour Cottage, probably scenting the evening air. James murmured in low tones through the lavatory door to Flynner, "Better watch out Flynner, I can see Ted Bollicks!" Within an instant, or so it seemed, Ted, whose hearing must have been as sharp as his salesmanship, was down the steps and had James by the throat, thrusting him back into the lavatory to crash against the door of the stall behind which Flynner was engaged in doing whatever he was engaged in doing.

Ted raved in James's face for a good few minutes, within the course of which he threatened a number of times to "wring your bloody ears!" In spite of the tirade James's main impression was of a poorly muffled attempt by Flynner to stifle his laughter from behind the shithouse door.

Ted's incandescence blocked out any sense he might otherwise have had of Flynner's near presence, and as he released his hold on James and stormed away back up the steps to Harbour Cottage, Ted never realised quite how close he had been to grabbing hold of someone he really wanted.

—

Ted made a regular extroverted presence in performances on the stage of the Temperance Hall. He had a gift for delivering jokes, but never quite managed to plumb the undernourished and worldly unwise depths of humour that might induce a Port Isaac audience to laugh.

Ted and Ruth once put on a double act of quips and gags that died as sure a death on the Temperance Hall stage as the comedians on the wireless always declared their own acts did at theatres in Glasgow. So much hilarity emerged in the retelling of

Ted and Ruth's debacle however, that their performance could be alleged to have achieved what it had originally set out to do, if indirectly.

———

Bollicks was only 14 years old when he died in Harbour Cottage after being bedridden for some weeks previously. The cause of his death was reported to be a burst blood vessel.

His funeral, held at St Endellion church, was the first funeral that many of his friends had ever attended. It was a morose affair. Roger Keat and James worked the organ pump for the hymns.

———

Bollicks deserved more from life than he got, but then again, who didn't?

The harbour at Port Quin

20

Words for All Seasons

LEONARD HONEY was a proper Port Isaac boy. He was a multi-attributed survivor. Although he suffered regularly from alarming attacks of asthma, Leonard always managed to recover from them at the exact moment when the boys who were with him at the time were looking at each other and thinking that this time he might not.

Among his contemporaries, Leonard's greatest claim to fame was an ability he possessed to swallow and instantly regurgitate large quantities of air. He could generate long, loud belches at will, some rumbling like passing thunder, others cracking out in a staccato rattle that would have done credit to a machine gun. Leonard's belches made windows rattle and tea ripple in cups sitting on the table. His friends, all of whom were less blessed than he, stood unfulfilled in the shadow of this immense talent.

For a while, the boys nicknamed Leonard "Ghandi", in the light of a striking resemblance that he bore to what in anyone's imagination could have been the emaciated Indian independence leader when he was a boy. However, Leonard was more familiarly known as "Buh", in an enshrinement of the first recognisable word he was alleged to have spoken as a baby, a valiant attempt to say "bugger". After that, the road to progress beckoned.

"Bugger" was a word in such comfortable and commonplace usage by Port Isaac men and women alike that it was inevitable that a growing baby like Leonard somewhere or other in the village would be drawn to cut his or her speaking ability on it.

"Bugger", in company with its equally beloved associate "bloody", was critical in maintaining the flow of any conversation. "Bloody" was pronounced as "bleddy", in a nuance of accent replacing bluntness with charm. These respective "B" words were laid as the twin foundation stones of communal vocabulary and were never invoked by their exponents with less than a dedicated sense of purpose.

"Bugger" was employed to replace just about any descriptive noun that could be thought of, or rather not thought of, as not thinking of a noun was the main reason for using "bugger" to replace it. Appropriately associated, "bugger" was quite capable of additionally forming an adjective, or better still, a verb. For its part, "bleddy" was mainly applied as a general adjective for all seasons.

The use of "bleddy" demanded access to neither a dictionary nor a thesaurus by its followers. It was understood to mean whatever it was intended to mean with all due consideration given to both context and tone of voice. Lewis Carroll's Humpty Dumpty would certainly have approved of the word "bleddy".

As an example of the encompassing scope of "bleddy", a comment on "the bleddy weather" could be understood to offer advice under pertinent circumstances that it was either too hot or too cold, or unpleasantly wet, or foggy, or maybe even windy. It could refer as much to last week's or last month's weather as it could to such weather as was prevalent today, and was quite able to project an appreciation of weather conditions into the future as well, probably more successfully than the weather forecasters on the wireless.

It didn't need a debate to establish that "bugger" was a rather more subtle word than "bleddy". "Bugger" was ringed about with so many delicate touches that it embraced a kaleidoscopic range of sentiments. Although women were as proficient as were men (and not forgetting the boys) in using the word "bugger", convention demanded that its prime subjective application was directed only towards masculine targets. A "little bugger", or better yet a "proper little bugger", always referred to a boy.

———

The "B" word "boy" was an additional form of conventional address applied in conversing with a member of the male sex irrespective of his age. "Boy" could be placed as a suffix at the end of any sentence. "All right, boy?" was the preferred way of asking men, from eight months to eighty years old and beyond, "How are you?"

The female equivalent was "maid", although the term tended to be disregarded for obvious reasons in the case of those unmarried ladies who had attained a certain age. Schoolgirls were more commonly described as "maidens".

———

Little buggers, or even proper little buggers, generally lost count of the number of times their elders and betters instructed them to "Bugger off!". Knowing what was good for them, such little buggers hastened to take the advice, and so buggered off, not hesitating to inform their elders and betters, once they were out of earshot that is, that as far as the little buggers who had buggered off were concerned their elders and betters could go to buggery.

———

A sudden surprise, pleasant or not, was sure to provoke in many Port Isaac men the exclamation "Well, I'll be buggered!". Some put it more simply as "Bugger me!". James's Gran Creighton, not given to using such expressions in the face of the unexpected, chose to give vent to "Oh, my gar!", and that served the very same purpose as being buggered did.

———

A "real bugger" defined an unpleasant individual or alternatively a tricky situation. Perhaps the greatest condemnation that could be wished on a specific individual however was that he was a "miserable bugger" or a "miserable old bugger". The esteem in which individuals so named were held was about as low as it could possibly be.

The majority of lists of personal likes and dislikes were sure to feature "big buggers", "real buggers", "silly buggers" and a whole host more. The highest accolade, the antithesis of a miserable old bugger, was reserved for "good buggers", or more especially, "good old buggers".

In cases in which heaping insult on injury was called for, and there were enough of those, the two "B" words were combined to place "bleddy buggers" on record.

Jim Honey, who was for his pains a distant uncle of Buh Honey, took the invocation of "bleddy buggers", as a term of rank invective, to heights that were probably never scaled before or would never be scaled again thereafter. Jim was a good old bugger who lived in a cottage with his sister Clara on Dolphin Street alongside Temple Bar. Clara, kindness made solid, looked after the short-fused Jim as best she could.

Jim was a fisherman from the top of his head to the soles of his feet. He was retired, and in his retirement he chose to break the mould of the standard Port Isaac fisherman's uniform black dress code by wearing a grey Guernsey in a touch of comparative colour. For all that, under a stained flat cap, with a rolling walk and a hand-rolled fag pasted damply in the corner of his mouth, Jim fit the balance of the fisherman's norm quite adequately.

Jim appeared to believe that very many people in very many places were out to do him down. He may have been right. All of those who wished him ill were, in Jim's considered view, a pack of "bleddy buggers", although Jim, the owner of a remarkable inability to use the letters "l" and "r" as God intended him to, pronounced the couplet "bweddy buggos". When Jim denounced the "bweddy buggos", in tones of pure gravel, he took no prisoners.

On Jim's list the parish council were bweddy buggos, the county council were bweddy buggos, all shopkeepers, all more successful fishermen than Jim had ever been, any visitors to Port Isaac, all of them were bweddy buggos of the first water conspiring against him and well deserving of his disdain. Jim may not always have been right, but then again, he was not always wrong either. The list of bweddy buggos was seemingly infinite.

———

Tim Scawin was a gentleman who undertook on a certain day to confront head on the use of the "B" words by some Port Isaac boys. Tim, a solicitor during the working week, lodged with the churchwarden Wesslick Brown and Wesslick's sister Alice in their pretty little cottage half way up Rose Hill. Neither Wesslick nor Alice (nor, supposedly Tim, let it be said) could remotely have been described, even by Jim Honey, as bweddy buggos.

Tim had possibly volunteered or perhaps had been impressed by Wesslick and Alice into teaching Sunday school at St Peter's, in which sideline he was very keen to suppress the prolific use of "B" words among the boys who were his charges. Tim acceded to the boys that there were occasions in life when it was necessary to give vent to stronger than usual exclamations, but when such occasions arose, Tim declared, they should be governed by absolute prudence.

"When I get upset", Tim advised the Sunday school class, "I always say 'Oh, pish!'"

"Do you now sir?" responded Michael Bate, faithful in his innocence to the last in the hallowed nave of St Peter's church, "I always do say 'Oh, bugger it!'"

———

Michael was a slow learner at school, but he was rapid enough on the uptake. Just like Jim Honey and Jim's namesake Buh, Michael could be described as a good old bugger without any fear of contradiction.

Michael's nickname was "Eyesnot". The nickname originated on a fateful day when some boys called on him at his house to come out and he told them "I's not coming". Eyesnot had a profound capacity for spitting and could summon up a gob of saliva to accompany every step he took. It was a miracle where all the spit came from.

On the occasion of his confirmation in St Peter's church, when Tim's teaching of the catechism was but a fading memory, Eyesnot stood in his allotted place in the line up of boys standing in front of the officiating Bishop of Truro. The bishop was an awesome presence. As he glided along the line in his crusted robes, he delivered a benediction to each boy in turn. If any of the boys felt infused by tongues of fire as a consequence, they hid their feelings well.

On reaching Eyesnot the bishop leaned over to whisper words in Eyesnot's ear, as if he had finally found a credible convert. Eyesnot dropped his hands and clasped them tightly in front of him.

Anxious to know what comfortable words the bishop saith unto Eyesnot, the rest of the newly confirmed boys went eagerly to Eyesnot following the ceremony, hoping that they might find enrichment in touching the hem of Eyesnot's coat. "Well", said Eyesnot, "The old bugger told me that me flies was undone".

The Bishop of Truro could well have rejoiced in being accorded old bugger status by one of the confirmed of Port Isaac.

Temple Bar, a street called strait

The Port Isaac valley and Top Shed

21

Old Egger

THE DWELLING PLACE of Mr Edgar Bate was a low-fronted cottage, firmly cramped into the tight line of residences that marked the lower half of the right hand side of Church Hill.

A sign at the top of Church Hill, set up at the precise point where the steep slope toppled gratefully over to become the flat onward road that wriggled around the hedges of fields towards Trelights and St Endellion, warned those who could read it that Church Hill was IMPRACTICABLE FOR MOTORS.

"Impracticable" was just about the longest word any of the Port Isaac boys had ever seen written on a sign. They pronounced the word out loud every time they passed the sign at the top of Church Hill, competing with each other as to who among them could puff out the string of hard consonants the loudest.

The boys liked that word. In a rare moment of academic enterprise, one of them consulted a dictionary to find out what the word meant and was gratified to learn that impracticable could easily be applied to most of the activities that the boys set out to perform. It was not that impracticability ever deterred them, even if it was perceived to confront them, as the boys generally succeeded in spite of themselves.

To emphasise the salutary advice to motorists arriving at the top of Church Hill from the direction of St Endellion, the sign additionally carried a big black triangle with the legend "1 in 5" beneath it. Suffice it to say that Church Hill was a steep hill.

In the days before St Peter's church was constructed, Church Hill was the weary route of pilgrimage trodden by the Church faithful on Sundays to attend services in the ancient, granite church at St Endellion.

———

Mr Edgar Bate's cottage was, perhaps fortuitously for him, not located on the most severely inclined section of Church Hill. The really steep part of Church Hill was related to its upper half, up above the old disused quarry. Nevertheless, any appreciably rounded object dropped on Church Hill outside Mr Edgar Bate's front door would in all probability still be able to roll rapidly all the way down to the Town Platt before finally calling it a day.

Residing with Mr Edgar Bate was his sister Fanny, a certain-aged spinster of this parish, and Mr Bernard Miller, a grizzled bachelor of this parish who may have been Edgar and Fanny Bate's lodger, or a special friend of either Mr Edgar Bate or of Fanny, or all of the above at the same time.

———

Bernard dabbled in farming. He worked a small field or two in the Port Isaac valley bottom just down below the old Mill, together with a much more extensive adjoining area of land occupying the precipitate slopes that fell away into the valley all along the rise of Church Hill.

Bernard's land holdings were grazed by a number of cattle and sheep. There may have been more than ten of each species hoofing it around his fields, but not many more than that. Bernard's sheep picked a delicate way across the valley-side field on tight tracks, seemingly concerned as much with remaining on their feet as in finding some decent grass to chew on.

A lonely crab apple tree, tall, twisted and tangled, had somehow taken root and endured in the centre of Bernard's valley slope field. The tree formed a focal point for sheep tracks to home in on. Beneath the thin branches of the tree stood an ancient horse, somnolent, its head hanging. The horse was a fixture of every-day permanence, although perhaps it struggled off elsewhere when night fell and no one could see it move.

———

Bernard's cattle barn down in the valley bottom had the great virtue of being two-floored. The Port Isaac boys knew the barn as "Top Shed". They gained access to the upper floor of Top Shed through a trapdoor, not always very conveniently as it happened since there was no ladder available. However, through a combination of bunking up and standing on each other's shoulders, the boys were always able to manage to pull themselves to the upper floor, one by one. Swallows nested in the eaves of Top Shed. There was no resident barn owl, but then, the boys couldn't have everything.

The one drawback to any occupancy of the upper floor of Top Shed by the boys was Bernard, who objected to their presence in a manner best described as antagonistic. The boys felt that any inherent risk was worth taking, however, and by posting a lookout for an incoming attack by Bernard when they were in Top Shed the boys made sure that Bernard couldn't get within striking distance of them. Although there were those times when Bernard did get within an uncomfortably close range, the boys were evasive targets, as slippery as the grey eels that slid through the sinuous currents of the lower Lake.

———

The boys always referred to Bernard's supposed landlord, Mr Edgar Bate, as "Old Edgar". Mr Edgar Bate was old, or at the very least he was getting old, so knowing him as Old Edgar was all right on that count for a start. In the case of Old Edgar, however, the given title of "Old" related primarily to the high level of affection in which the boys held him.

The boys regarded Old Edgar as a good man who was their friend. A lot of men were less than tolerant of boys in general for a host of reasons, some of which were reasonably justified and some of which were not. Old Edgar was not like those men. He

209

met the boys on their own terms and he did not patronise them. They liked that.

—

On his head, Old Edgar wore a black, low-crowned trilby hat. The hat sat flat and square and looked as crushed as if Old Edgar had slept in it. For all the boys knew, that was exactly what Old Edgar did, as they never saw him, even sitting down inside his home, without he had his hat on at full mast.

Old Edgar's face was adorned with a long, grey, drooping moustache, stained dull brown along its dangling wisps by a lip-seeping residue that dribbled from the stem of the curved pipe that was invariably clamped between his dentures.

His most characteristic physical feature was vested in his right leg, which was significantly shorter than his left leg. This would not have been a bad asset for prowling in one specific direction across Bernard's valley-side field, but as Old Edgar didn't seem to be one to involve himself in the farming side of Bernard's activities it was an asset that never came to be tested.

Old Edgar made his way around with commendable efficiency, aided by a compensating wooden crutch, polished through use, jammed up under his right arm so tightly that it might have been growing there. All that was missing, thought the boys, was a bright parrot to sit on Old Edgar's shoulder and scream "*Pieces of eight!*"

—

Old Edgar's two great attributes for enduring fame as far as the boys were concerned were his collections of postage stamps and of birds' eggs. His postage stamp collection was rumoured to contain stamps whose great variety and number were matched by its value. Old Edgar had once worked as a postman. What he didn't know about postage stamps wasn't worth knowing.

He was always ready to show one or other of his precisely maintained stamp albums to the boys who visited him. Old Edgar's stamp albums bulged with neatly hinged rows of stamps in bright colours, exotic designs, wild animals and strange faces emanating from all around the British Empire and whatever else was left of the limited world outside it.

The boys nodded their appreciation of the stamps they saw, wishing in some cases that they were really as impressed as they ought to have been.

—

Stamp collections were commenced by many of the boys with a frequency that was as great as the life of such collections was short. As often as not the platform used for stamp collecting was the acquisition by post of stamp "approvals", as advertised in the weekly comics.

The general idea behind the stamp approval system was that stamps were sent by gullible suppliers to cunning applicants to be bought or sold on to others by the applicants, who were then required to forward the full proceeds (or return unsold stamps) to the supplier in the form of a postal order. To offer the opinion in the post-war Port Isaac context that this was a process doomed to failure would be to severely understate the case.

—

The boys were quite prepared to sit through the preliminaries of Old Edgar's presentation of stamp albums in order to get to the top of the bill inspection of his collection of birds' eggs. These, understood to have been all gathered by Old Edgar's own hand, were considered by the boys to represent a prize second to none.

Old Edgar's birds' eggs were carefully arranged, resting securely in neat wooden boxes on mats of sawdust. They were graded for size, colour and intensity of markings. Just about every type of bird's egg that could possibly have been obtained in and around the parish, and up and down the cliffs of Port Isaac Bay, was represented in those treasure trove boxes.

—

"Birds' egging" or "birds' nesting" was an activity pursued by the majority of the boys with a level of enthusiasm that made it their prime seasonal activity. Birds' egging was totally competitive. It generated an intense rivalry between the boys during the nesting season in seeking out birds' nests, obtaining the first bird's egg, and understanding where the most desirable eggs could be found.

First egg of the season! (Sang the boys.)
O! What a surprise!
We didn't think we'd get one!
But we're telling lies!

In its season, birds' egging was the quintessential outdoor pursuit, with established, if unwritten, rules. For its proponents birds' egging developed a detailed expertise, gathered at first hand, of nesting habitats, species identification, construction of nests, average numbers of eggs laid per species, and the duration of breeding seasons.

The practice of birds' egging was not strictly catered for within the letter of the law, but the Port Isaac policeman, Mr Pearce, who lived in a picture postcard cottage at Trewetha, generally ignored the practice as long as the unwritten rules were followed to the unwritten letter.

—

Mr Pearce was an archetypal village policeman: solid, square, fair and just, trusted and much admired. Unfortunately it was not possible for the same to be said by the boys about Mr Pearce's later successors on the Port Isaac beat.

One day in birds' egging season Mr Pearce met up with a small group of boys who, given the time of year and the place of the encounter, had clearly been birds' egging.

On perceiving the approach of Mr Pearce, the boys placed the birds' eggs that each of them had taken on top of their respective heads under their caps, so as to hide the bounty from Mr Pearce's view. They were, for once, carrying no bulky cotton wool filled egg-collecting tins to give the game away.

"Well boys", said Mr Pearce, "have you been birds' egging?"

"Oh no, Mr Pearce!" came their virtuous reply.

"Good boys!" said Mr Pearce, patting each one heavily on his cap-covered head, before moving on at his customarily steady pace just as the first trickle of yolk appeared from under the caps and ran on down the faces of those good boys.

Old Edgar's birds' egg collection was a masterpiece. There was nothing that the boys who saw it either owned or envisaged owning in their whole lives that they would not have given away immediately and unconditionally to obtain a birds' egg collection like it. It stimulated and excited their imagination and it generated in them tenth commandment breaking feelings of covetousness.

Such was the magical quality of old Edgar's birds' egg collection that for a long while the boys who viewed the collection so avariciously believed that old Edgar's name was really old "Egger", and they pronounced his name accordingly.

Old Edgar sat at home, puffing away at his pipe, wearing a stained black jacket, even more stained black trousers and a once white shirt. The shirt was collarless but had a redundant collar stud always in place ready for a collar to arrive in the unlikely event that Fanny would be able to locate a clean collar.

Old Edgar's physical disability was no drawback to him in climbing either trees or cliffs. His crutch served as a third leg as he moved with a jerky grace along the cliff tops, where he was as sure footed as a rabbit.

A permanent memento of Old Edgar's prime egg collecting days was a truncated finger on his right hand. The missing section of the finger was surgically removed by a puffin that objected to Old Edgar's hand being thrust down the burrow it was resident in out at Varley Head.

On that celebrated occasion Edgar might well have lost a finger joint, but he did gain the fair trade of a puffin's egg, which he would readily point out in one of his birds' egg collection boxes to any boy who asked him about it.

On the stile above Lobber Field

From left to right: James Platt, Michael Collings, Terry Thomas, David Sloggett

22

Run, Rabbit, Run Rabbit, Run, Run, Run

ALL ALONG THE CLIFF TOPS, bouncy tussocks of grass, slickly undulate, ranged one on the other like a miniature cockpit of wind-trained hillocks. Great rounded bursts of sea pinks added greater relief to the array and marched onwards to invade the hedges of cliff-side fields in a benign flurry.

Countless rabbit burrows, excavated by as many generations of rabbits without count, riddled this green sward, making of it a spongy mass that yielded to the feet of cliff walkers, sometimes alarmingly. Turning an ankle was an ever-present possibility for any inexperienced itinerant who elected not to keep one good weather eye on the ground ahead of him.

The rabbit population of the parish contributed a vital element to the staple diet of Port Isaac residents. A rabbit held the advantage of being available for dropping into a cooking pot (suitably dead, skinned and gutted of course) at any time of the year.

If the numbers of rabbits living out along the cliffs and up in the valleys, and all through the fields and under the woods, had not been kept in some kind of check by means of their steady incorporation as ingredients in various stews and assorted pies, their uncontrolled host would in all probability have overrun the parish and driven the people of the parish to seek refuge elsewhere.

215

There were just so very many rabbits. Not absolutely too many, mind you, as there could never be absolutely too many. As it was, anyone peering over almost any hedge and looking into almost any field anywhere around Port Isaac could do so in the confident expectation that there would be more rabbits in his view than could be counted in a hurry, assuming that he knew how to count without recourse to his fingers.

The rabbit population was blasted by guns, shot at by catapults, ginned by farmers, chased by boys, snared by all and sundry and hunted down by dogs, cats, ferrets, foxes, owls and buzzards. Yet, for all this entire endeavour to decimate the ranks, the rabbit multitude was barely dented.

Wild rabbits had somehow, by a likely miracle of subterfuge, managed to work their way into interbreeding with their domesticated captive rabbit cousins. Not infrequently along the open cliffs where the absence of arboreal cover permitted rabbits to be seen more readily, splashes of white, black and red fur might well enhance the standard palette of monotonic feral grey brown.

Cliff dwelling rabbits were the specialists of their breed. They were swift and sure-footed. In order to access isolated patches of greenery they scuttled boldly along precarious ledges that appeared to afford the minimum of foothold. In the manner of the vegetation, the rabbits held a sound purchase on the cliff faces against the odds.

Rabbits were shot at, and usually but not always hit, with an arsenal of arms ranging from twelve-bore and .410 shotguns to .22 calibre rifles and various air rifles and pistols. Such weaponry was in widespread use.

A boy could obtain a BSA or Diana air rifle or a Webley air pistol by making a simple response, enclosing the all-important postal order, to an advertisement for the same in one or other of the weekly comics. A handsome weapon, just as ordered, was subsequently delivered directly by the postman to the lucky recipient's home. Armed thus, in the course of an evening stroll through a field or two, a boy could bag a couple of rabbits with no great effort.

———

Farmers favoured catching rabbits by setting up lines of rabbit gins both around the verges of their fields and along established tracks that they had identified as rabbit runs. A rabbit gin was a steel device a foot or so long. It was armed with a set of viciously toothed, hinged jaws at one end, worked by a stiff spring clip that formed the main body of the instrument. A long spike, to peg the gin down firmly and so prevent it being dragged away by a trapped bunny, was attached to the gin by a length of chain.

To open the formidable jaws the spring clip was pushed down, and the jaws were then locked in a ready position around a hinged pressure plate. The least touch on the pressure plate would cause the jaws to instantly snap shut with crushing force around whatever portion of a rabbit's anatomy had made the contact.

The farmers pegged the rabbit gins into the ground at regular intervals along the selected rabbit-travelled routes. Each gin was carefully dug in and then disguised under a light dusting of soil. In principle any passing rabbit stepping on the pressure plate would have its most unlucky foot grabbed by the steel jaws and would there be held for eventual despatch when the farmer made his next visit to check the gin line.

———

On their wanderings through the valleys and fields the Port Isaac boys were no strangers to the cruel results of rabbit ginning practice. It was impossible for some of the boys, primarily those fortunate enough to be unrelated to farmers and their working philosophy, to reconcile in their minds how the use of rabbit gins could be held consistent with the morals of a village society that cowered, bible or prayer book in hand, beneath either a church or a chapel umbrella with such impressive piety.

Rabbit gins certainly trapped rabbits, but they mangled rabbit limbs in the process and caused the creatures an unacceptable immensity of suffering. Additionally, gins had no discrimination on what they caught. Cats, dogs, foxes and even badgers were as vulnerable to gins as were rabbits. The boys had seen all of this.

James and his friend Roger Keat took a vehement dislike to the practice of rabbit ginning. When they were out and chanced to come across a setting of rabbit gins, they followed the line along and sprang each gin with a stick. ("Out" was what they told their mothers when their mothers asked them where they were going. "Out" was understood to cover all parts and corners of the parish, and was descriptive enough never to require any additional elaboration.)

James's and Roger's gin-springing activity became a virtual crusade, and they eventually took up the practice of going out on expeditions with the sole objective of finding and springing as many rabbit gins as possible.

One extended line of a couple of score or more of rabbit gins was set along the exposed hill crest above Roscarrock Hill and Church Hill. The line stretched from the edge of Lobber in a long and gentle curve around to the lip of Hancock's quarry. James and Roger sprang that line a number of times, until James –since Roger wasn't identified – was spotted by an observant farmer looking up at the hill crest from downtown Port Isaac.

The observant farmer, who remained as anonymous as such informers usually do, reported the matter to the then village policeman, a successor (once removed following the short-lived career of P. C. Thomas) to Mr Pearce. The name of this policeman was P. C. Dyer, and naturally enough the boys called him Diarrhoea as he was a fair bit of a shit to them.

Diarrhoea visited the primary school to interview James in connection with the reported crime. It was common enough for

218

any alleged offenders to be interviewed by Diarrhoea in this way. For a start, Diarrhoea could always be sure to locate whomsoever he wanted, as no one ever missed going to school.

Outside school hours Diarrhoea generally called on his suspects at their homes. The principle behind such encounters, whether in or out of school, was that the suspect was guilty until proved innocent, not only in the opinion of Diarrhoea but also in that of the suspect's teachers, parents and neighbours. The arrival of Diarrhoea at a cottage in any street set neighbourly curtains twitching and tongues wagging in parallel waves.

On being extracted from class to meet Diarrhoea, although with no regrets on James's part for missing the lesson that had been proceeding at the time, it was to have Diarrhoea inform James that he was guilty of a serious offence that could merit a spell for him in a place that Diarrhoea referred to as Borstal. Whatever or wherever Borstal was, was never adequately clarified to James.

Diarrhoea demanded to know who James's unidentified accomplice was in the gin-springing incident. One thing James knew for sure, from reading *Adventure* and *The Hotspur* (among other impeccable sources of information on how he should comport himself), was that giving away the names of his friends to people in authority was not an honourable thing to do. James therefore declined to advise Diarrhoea of anything.

Since James and Roger were known to be inseparable companions, James could imagine that even someone as obdurate as Diarrhoea could have hazarded an educated guess as to precisely whom James was refusing to name.

Diarrhoea's immediate reaction was to inform James that a refusal to name his partner in crime had at once made the nature of the crime even more serious. If James persisted in this attitude when (not if) he appeared in court, Diarrhoea told him, he would be held to be in contempt. James didn't really know what contempt meant in that context, so the threat bounced balloon-like off him. The only contempt that he felt at that particular moment was directed at Diarrhoea.

———

James's elders and betters were then consulted, and they were advised by Diarrhoea that James had given him a classic "mouthful of cheek". This was really bearing false witness, as James felt he had been most polite with Diarrhoea at all times. On the other hand, any attempt at self-expression that he could make was, by convention, certain to be deemed a mouthful of cheek at whomsoever it was directed.

Under growing pressure, James buckled in and named Roger. It was a matter of enormous shame for him, even if it seemed that that really was the end of the matter, as the whole affair faded away overnight. However, there was still a lesson to be learned by James and Roger, and the lesson was that they needed to take much more care in future not to be observed in the act of springing rabbit gins.

———

When the farmers cut the corn in their fields in the late summer, the fields swarmed with human activity. Cutting the corn commenced in a corner of the selected field. The corn cutter, drawn by a pair of horses or a motor-driven tractor if there was one, worked around the field in a inwardly spiralling route drawing ever more tightly towards the centre.

Many untrained and impressively inexpert hands were brought in or simply turned up to work with the regular farm labourers in conducting the corn cutting process. Sometimes the newcomers genuinely did help, but as often as not they hindered, all with the best of grace of course.

The cut corn was gathered and tied into bundles or "shocks", which were subsequently stacked upright in individual groups of three or four for maturing and drying in the cleared part of the field. Some mechanical corn cutters were able to bind the shocks automatically with rough, hairy twine.

A field spotted with stacked shocks of corn was an inviolate symbol of the harvest time. A few special corn shocks were selected for decorating St Peter's church and both Methodist chapels for the Harvest Festival services.

———

As the corn cutter ran its ever-decreasing course around the field, the many resident rabbits, rats and mice, deprived of cover, moved into the closing eye of uncut corn. Once in a while an occasional rabbit would attempt to make a break for freedom through the strung out gauntlet of men and boys busily stacking corn shocks. Few rabbits got through. If the men didn't drop a fleeing rabbit with a well aimed stone, a thrust from a pitchfork, or for that matter with their bare hands, then dogs, waiting expectantly, would be sure to do so. Any rabbit taken alive was immediately despatched by a chopping blow, a "rabbit punch", across the back of its neck with the edge of a calloused labouring hand.

Ultimately the shrinking circle of standing corn in the field would reach a critical dimension. A panicked horde of rabbits, with more than a few rats and mice keeping them company, then boiled *en masse* out of the remaining corn, dodging, leaping and racing in every direction to achieve the safety of the surrounding hedges. A lot of rabbits made it through, but many didn't. The toll of the fallen was heavy.

This was *"Run, rabbit, run rabbit, run, run, run"* in action, as Messrs Flanagan and Allen, given the least excuse to do so, were happy to sing. When the working day had finished with either all the corn cut or the sun about to set, whichever came sooner, the day's catch of rabbits was shared between the workers, helpers and hinderers alike, and the imminent prospect of a rabbit pie on many tables once again reared its lip-smacking head.

———

To remove the skin from a rabbit it was first of all necessary to cut off the head and make a downward slit to open the rabbit up from the neck to the base of the belly with a sharp knife. The innards were then scooped out with one motion of the skinner's hand. After that, with a swift and clean drag from the neck the skin was peeled backwards with a squishy, tearing sound to expose the translucent purplish red meat of the rabbit carcass.

Slits were made all around the feet and the tail to permit the rabbit skin to be removed in a single piece. A rabbit skin was usually discarded, although the fur had a pleasing softness to it and was sometimes tanned and made into garments, usually by gypsies, and employed perhaps for wrapping up Baby Bunting.

———

Certain individuals elected to retain a rabbit's foot as a lucky charm, in which capacity the object was used to satisfy a basic desire that it might bring more luck to the owner of the charm than it had ultimately provided for the rabbit from which it was taken.

Since the art of embalming or otherwise curing a rabbit's foot as an item of personal vanity was not especially advanced in Port Isaac, what the possession of such an item brought to the pocket of its new owner, apart from the forlorn anticipation of luck, was a not especially appealing odour. But then again, one more such smell attaching itself to so many others of an equally redolent personal ilk, didn't make a whole lot of difference.

———

It was most common to consume a rabbit in a dismembered state in a pie or in a stew. The former was more or less a version of the latter, with the difference that a pie came with the advantage of having a slab of pastry on top to hide the ingredients from view.

The ingredients, apart from bits of rabbit, were whatever was available to hand at the time of cooking. Potato, cabbage, carrot, parsnip, turnip (white or swede), broccoli, cauliflower and sprouts all were fair game in a rabbit pie. By virtue of overcooking, the vegetables were induced to disintegrate and merge together to form a thick mush. The rabbit flesh dropped away from the bones in succulent shreds.

The pastry covering a pie was as unique a product as were the fingerprints of the pastry maker. There were a host of closely guarded pastry recipes. Most were retained in the head of the maker and few were ever committed to the written word on paper. Preparing good pastry was a knack which some had and many didn't have. It was an individual skill, often although not always handed down from generation to generation. The taste, texture, crispness, softness, toughness or propensity for mastication of a wedge of pastry could immediately specify the identity of its maker.

———

The rabbit cornucopia of the parish was, however, sadly destined not to last forever.

———

One day, in the very early 1950s James, Roger (not surprisingly) and Eyesnot Bate came across a large rabbit crouched low in the grass up on the crest of the Port Gaverne valley. The rabbit made no attempt to run away from them. They walked right up to it and they could touch it and still it remained motionless.

A sharp odour rose from the rabbit, not dissimilar to that which, in the boys' experience, surrounded the noisome external urinal of the Golden Lion. The rabbit's head was grossly deformed. There were bulbous pink swellings covering its eyes, which were closed to weeping slits.

This was the boys' first encounter with what they came to regard as the ultimate horror of the rabbit plague known as myxomatosis. The plague was an outrage visited by farmers upon the countryside as a means of curbing, not to say wiping out, the rabbit population.

———

Myxomatosis originated, so it was later understood, somewhere in France. So contagious and sweeping was myxomatosis that it virtually extinguished rabbits from the parish in the course of a season. The foul odour of the diseased and the rotting rabbit dead lay over the land like a cloud.

The arrival of myxomatosis in the Port Isaac area sounded the death knell for rabbit pies. An occasional rabbit was still offered up for sale, suspiciously enough always decapitated, but there were no takers for rabbit meat any more. Everyone soon came to know what a "myxy" rabbit looked like. A great door was slammed shut in nature, diminishing all who were there to feel the tremor of the reverberation.

———

For all that it was so severely interrupted, nature moved on and adjusted, as it always did. The grass that rabbits had formerly cropped short grew damp and lank. Foxes, deprived of a key diet, became wide-ranging scavengers and elected to raid farmyards to prey on chickens, as did buzzards as well, which served the farmers right in the opinion of the boys.

The Trefreock Valley above Pine Awn

Port Gaverne

23

The Carol Singers

NONE OF THE PORT ISAAC BOYS wanted the summer holidays to end, but end they always did. Once the summer holidays were over the boys had to go back to school. However, they were comforted in the knowledge that they could then begin ticking off, one by one, a seemingly interminable list of Trinity Sundays in a burgeoning anticipation of eventually reaching the haven of the first Advent Sunday.

The long and rocky desert path through the mighty month (well, twenty-five days anyway, which was near enough) of Trinity Sundays was agreeably eased for the boys by the intervention of Guy Fawkes Day.

Guy Fawkes Day rolled up on them like a November the fifth oasis. The boys called the day "Guy Fox Day". A bonfire by any other name would have burned as sweet.

The preparations that went into making a success of Guy Fox Day created a curling wave of excitement. The collection, by fair means or foul, of combustible household rubbish for the great bonfire, the construction of poor old Guy Fox in effigy, the parade of Guy Fox's effigy through the streets of Port Isaac in the forlorn hope by Guy Fox's bearers that their plaintive request "A penny for the Guy?" would be heeded by members of the public, and the constant plotting of ways and means of acquiring some fireworks (especially bangers) in the absence of the wherewithal to buy them, were not the least of such preparations.

———

When Guy Fox had had his day, and when all that was left of his cited effigy was a mere part of a smouldering ring of mournful ashes at the head of the harbour beach, the solace of the count-down to Advent 1 was instantly taken up once more.

With Advent 1 an almost tangible reality, the boys were happy in the knowledge that a key milestone in their lives was close to hand. The mighty goal of Christmas on the other side of Advent 1 could at last begin to engage with all their senses simultaneously. The past summer as seen from that perspective might have been good to look back on, but there was nothing like the anticipation of a Christmas coming to stir the blood.

Experience taught the boys that the real thrill of Christmas was very much vested in the conduct of the build-up to the big day. That day itself was always going to be worth reaching, but it fell as flat as a pancake when it finally arrived. It was the road towards Christmas, hopefully travelled, that made Christmas all that it ought to be.

———

On the brink of Advent 1, there were some urgent requirements that needed to be tackled.

For a start there was the matter of holly. The boys had an inti-mate knowledge of all the woods and valleys of the parish and beyond and so were well aware of the locations of all the extant holly trees and bushes. In the general course of most of their year they ignored the incidence of holly. No bird ever built a nest in a holly tree, a fact that eliminated in an instant any desire the boys might have felt to penetrate the prickly barrier to search within.

Holly sprigs and branches as such were always easy to obtain, assuming that those who obtained them were happy to come up with holly leaves alone. That was the problem with holly trees. To suit Christmas, holly trees needed to bear berries as red as any blood. That in the overwhelming majority of cases around Port Isaac holly trees didn't bear berries at all was a cause of great frustration. No self-respecting boy wanted to take home any holly devoid of berries.

There was always berried holly to be found somewhere or other, but the job was to find out where that somewhere or other was, and moreover to be the first to get to it. Scouting expeditions for berried holly ranged the length and breadth of the Port Isaac and Port Gaverne valleys, and when they were unsuccessful, as they invariably were that close to home, the boys crossed watersheds and the parish boundary to spread their eager net as far and as wide as was necessary.

Given the shortness of the late autumn days, finds of berried holly were generally brought along into Port Isaac at a time of darkness. The berried holly was received with acclaim by the authorities of St Peter's church, the two chapels and the homes that it would bless and decorate for Christmas. If the vicar's enthusiasm for the gift of berried holly was not quite shared in kind by the farmer from whose land the holly was taken, the vicar never seemed to let it concern him, much to his credit.

———

The prospect of approaching Christmas induced James's Gran Creighton to hunt down and retrieve, from the place where they were put away and nearly but not quite forgotten about following last Christmas, the prized pair of nutcrackers that only ever emerged into God's good daylight at Christmas time. The pair of nutcrackers was a wonderfully lethal instrument that was absolutely guaranteed to shatter any variety of nut into a myriad of pieces and to spray every corner of a room and its occupants with shelly shrapnel. The heel of a shoe was much to be preferred for cracking nuts.

———

In most homes a venerable but priceless cardboard box of time-honoured Christmas decorations was brought down from an attic to be sorted out and readied again for distribution over Christmas trees, cottage walls and ceilings. The tangle of last year's paper chains was unravelled to the extent that it was possible. Flour paste was concocted to repair chain links where they had come adrift and to install new links on the chain where they were needed.

────

At the precise moment that the boys felt able to judge that it was no longer too early in December (even though it was inevitably early enough, as the early bird was reckoned to be the one that caught the worm) they commenced their rounds of carol singing from door to door around Port Isaac, moving about like the berried holly under a cloak of darkness.

It was appropriate to call the roaming groups of carol singers Legion, for they were many. They were locked in a competition for recompense for their vocal efforts that was quite as keen in its commission as the harmonies of the ill-rendered carols they sang were deaf in tone.

In their rendering of favourite carols, the boys came to epitomise what Charlie Chester intended in the "Crime Reporter" sketch of his famous wireless programme *Stand Easy* when Charlie claimed that "Once again a popular tune is murdered at the piano".

────

The description of the boys as "carol singers", although technically accurate, tended to place a holly leaf-like gloss on the talent of the boys to perform. The reality was not the substance of the holly leaf but the prickles that surrounded it. Their style was to attack the lines and fill in words they either didn't know or had otherwise forgotten, with whatever words came immediately to mind.

A carol-singing group was kept small, usually three in number, or at the most four. The restriction was essential in order to ensure a maximum gain to each member of the group at the final share-out of the proceeds extorted from cottage holders. Many cottage holders appeared relieved enough to hand a coin or two over to banish carol-singing boys from their doorsteps in the hope that this would prevent the boys ever returning.

These unwitting cottage holders were slow to realise that once the colour of their money and their apparent willingness to part with it was made plain, their cottage doors became an instant magnet for future attention by the boys. A generous cottage holder could count on repeated visits, in the course of which the carol-singing boys were puzzled to discover how quickly a one-time Dr Jekyll benefactor could transform into a Mr Hyde.

———

In principle the rules of carol singing were simple enough. The process began with an exploratory knock on a selected door. In the event that anyone came to the door, a polite request was made as to whether or not those who dwelt within wished to have a carol (or two) sung to them by the would-be carol singers. An acceptance resulted in a carol (or two) sung for the optional payment of a small fee. A refusal called for a dignified withdrawal by the carol singers.

That was the principle. In practice, like all tried and true practices, it didn't work quite like that. The polite request was out for a start, so as to avoid any option of refusal. The carol singing began without any recognisable preliminaries.

The first knock on the door was made following the singing of no more than two verses of the first carol. If no one responded from within, one or two verses of a second carol might be tried as an inducement to attract attention. The door knocking was then picked up both in frequency and volume until the cottage holder came along either to pay up or to chase the carol singers away.

When it was known there were people inside the cottage who were demonstrating no perceptible intention of emerging to hand over coins (a technique of concealment they would have learned in conjunction with the visits of their rent man), versions of well-known carols using updated lyrics were thrown out as a challenge to provoke a reaction by the miserly.

A recalcitrant cottage holder could anticipate being treated perhaps first to a rendition of we three Kings of holly and tar, one of whom was in a taxi and one in a car. The other was on a scooter blowing his hooter, as they were following yonder star. Or they could be regaled with the carol in which wild shepherds washed their socks by night and obtained heavenly assistance from a bar of Sunlight soap. Better still was the saga of good King Wenceslas, who on the feast of Stephen, turned his trousers inside out to keep his ass from freezing.

But it was with harking the herald angels that the last throw of the dice was done before a frustrated departure made without benediction.

> *Hark! The herald angels sing,*
> *Beecham's Pills are just the thing.*
> *If you want to go to heaven,*
> *You must take six or seven.*
> *If you want to go to hell,*
> *You must take the box as well.*

With a final thunderous knock on the door of the miserably cheap buggers whose doorstep they had until then honoured with their presence, the carol singers slunk away into the night in search of their next potential victim. That is, unless they left in more of a hurry with an irate cottage holder in hot pursuit.

Peace on earth then reigned again for a while. Goodwill to men really depended on the number and denomination of coins handed over to the carol singers imbued with their own interpretation of the spirit of Christmas.

The Port Gaverne Valley with Pendogget on the skyline

St Endellion church

24

The Christmas Party

THE ST PETER'S CHURCH Sunday school Christmas party always took place in the main hall of the Church Rooms. The party was celebrated slightly ahead of Christmas Day proper, in which capacity it did much to promote both the religious and the burgeoning secular spirits of the season.

To make space for the festivities, the bigger items of PT Club equipment were ignominiously shoved away in a corner of the hall. Shaky trestle tables, and even shakier chairs, were then set up in great longitudinal lines on the splintery wooden floor of the hall to respectively bear the weight of the repast and endure the individual weights of all those who were to be the beneficiaries.

The party feast consisted of as many sandwiches, buns, jellies and trifles as any Sunday school pupil could realistically shake a hymnbook at and which, at the time, made life just about as good as it could be. The feast was irrigated in the main by a seemingly limitless flow of good strong, dark tea, defying connoisseurs of the brew to declare that they could piddle stronger than that. (Although no doubt there were some that could perform that feat.) In addition, liquid refreshment incorporated a rather more sparing volume of coloured and mildly flavoured water that masqueraded as pop.

The tea was brewed in a mighty urn of radiantly hot and shiny metal that held its steaming pride of place within the anteroom to the Church Rooms. The anteroom was off limits to all except for the gaggle of ladies who prepared the tea and assembled certain of the party refreshments within. This association led some of the boys to think of the anteroom as an "anti room", or alternatively, an "aunty room".

———

Christmas as such owed its spirit to the attitude of mind with which it was approached, aided by the build-up and the sense of anticipation that was generated by the growing proximity of the season. Along the heartening path leading to Christmas Day there was, on the face of it at any rate, a readiness for people to smile a little more often than was their normal grim-faced custom. The feeling of well-being that infused the first three weeks of December was so much more satisfying than the realisation of Christmas Day itself, when any prior buoyancy in the atmosphere inevitably fell as flat as a punctured tyre.

———

At the Sunday school Christmas party the walls and roof beams in the hall of the Church Rooms were bright with coloured crepe paper decorations. Glossy green holly leaves adorned with blood-red berries, attached to every vantage point that could be reached with or without the assistance of a stepladder, gleamed where the light caught them.

All those attending the party were enveloped in an ultimate flood tide of cheer as they pulled crackers, scrabbling for the flimsy paper hats the crackers contained, and roaring with laughter as the cracker-borne jokes were read out one by one. The more venerable and weaker the joke, the greater was the communal guffaw it gave rise to.

———

The party gathering was clattering, yelling and exceedingly boisterous. Over its tumult, an angel of conviviality was sure to be spreading wide and caring wings. Or so the vicar said. Crumbs flew, drink was spilled, and bits of bread were thrown. Some boy pulled some girl's pigtails in a fit of exuberance and received an equally exuberant smack in the gob for his trouble. Others crawled under the trestles, or over the trestles, or ran around the trestles in an opportunistic search for delicacies that had already become extinct in the vicinity of reach where the perpetrators of the hunt were originally seated.

When the bun fight finally wound down the trestle tables were moved with great despatch to the sides of the hall, hands shifting them as eagerly as if the director of activities was none other than Mr Fezziwig. The floor of the hall was then an open battlefield on which the party games could commence.

—

As often as not, the first game to take place was "Musical chairs". This was designed not only to get the participants all hustling and bustling together at the same time but also to ensure that that particularly ferocious and competitive game would be safely out of the way early on in the proceedings, when it could, perhaps, still be controlled.

Every participant in the game of musical chairs was in the game with a positive determination that he or she would not be the only one left standing without a seat on which to park his or her backside when the music stopped. More than a few of those who were eliminated were not unlikely to object to their elimination in very strong terms and were quite prepared to fight off any challengers for the right to sit down. Most games of musical chairs involved at least one rolling brawl, and hopefully more than one if the luck held out.

—

With "Musical chairs" over, and any altercations patched up by compulsory, if reluctant, handshakes (although there was always next years fight to look forward to), the party games took on a more even-tempered passage with "Pass the parcel", "Blind man's buff", "Simon says" and "How green you are", conducted under the benevolent eye of the vicar together with the very many mothers who were first and foremost there for the tea and only thereafter for the cause (already lost) of keeping order.

———

The games session concluded with a spirited "Okey-cokey", involving everyone in the hall, including the vicar. All present linked arms in a wavering oval that went all the way around the perimeter of the hall, and sang through the sequence of the "Okey-cokey" for as long as their stamina lasted. They danced forwards and backwards, and to and fro from the walls into the centre, surging like waves against rocks, and draining out in retreat in the same way.

The rules of the "Okey-cokey" were implicit in the words that everyone knew so well:

> *You put your left leg in,*
> *Your left leg out!*
> *In-out, in-out,*
> *Shake it all about!*
> *You do the Okey-cokey*
> *And you turn around,*
> *Ant that's what it's all about!*
> *Hey!*
>
> *Ooooooooooh do the Okey-cokey!*
> *Oooooooooooooooooh do the Okey-cokey!*
> *Oooooooooooooooooooooooooh do the Okey-cokey!*
> *Knees bend, arms bend!*
> *Clap, clap, clap!*

The "*Ooooooooooh*" chorus formed the trigger to a unified inward rush of the ring of participants.

A left-leg verse was followed by a right-leg verse, and then came a left arm, a right arm and a head or a shoulder. Whereas in principle no item of anatomy was excluded from the "Okey-

238

cokey", in practice there were one or two that didn't get put in and shaken all about, perhaps in deference to the vicar's presence.

———

The highlight of the St Peter's Sunday school Christmas party was the presentation of annual prizes. The prize giving ceremony took place following the termination of the games, probably in order to ensure that most of the prizes awarded would survive the subsequent celebrations intact, and thereby to further deter the use of the prizes as available weapons of assault during the more lively party moments.

The underlying philosophy behind successive Sunday school prizes was that after a period of years the pupil would have been presented with a number of key props to cement his or her continuing church membership, among which would be a Bible, a personal crucifix, and a Book of Common Prayer incorporated with Hymns Ancient and Modern. After all that it might be possible to change tack on the style of prize – well, perhaps.

To illustrate this noble and most moral intent, the sequence of James's Sunday school prizes was a good example.

1945   *Listen to a Little Child – a book of thoughts for children's worship, being Part 1 of the Children's Prayer Book* by the Rev. G. R. Harding-Wood M.A.

1946   *Saints who spoke English* by Joan Wyndham, illustrated by Kathleen Cooper.

1947   *The Children's Life of Christ* by Enid Blyton, illustrated by Eileen Soper.

1948   *The New Testament.*

1949   A wooden crucifix on which was mounted a plastic figure of Jesus.

1950   *The Holy Bible.*

1951   *Biggles – Charter Pilot* by Capt. W. E. Johns.

1952   *The Valley of Mystery* by Capt. Oswald Dallas.

1953   *Stuart in Tibet* by Neil Buckley.

1954   *Moby Dick* by Herman Melville.

———

James somehow managed to miss out on being presented with a combined Book of Common Prayer and Hymns A&M, although in any case such a volume was available for him to borrow, free of charge, at all church services. The rest of the scheduled items were awarded on cue. The only misfortune to occur was that the plastic Jesus fell off his wooden cross and got lost before he could be stuck back on. It was not certain when he fell off exactly, but it happened a lot more than three days after James got him.

—

The various novels that James received as prizes, once his Bible was secured, were all, with the exception of *Moby Dick*, marked by clean-cut heroes and a high moral tone.

Although he many times took up the novels to read, he was unable to pretend to have finished any of them, apart from *Biggles – Charter Pilot*. That book contained a set of short stories about Biggles and his pals Algy and Ginger. The stories were too short really, as well as being very thin on plot, and it required a dedicated effort for him to plod through them.

A much more exciting Biggles book, a full novel this time, *Biggles in the Baltic* was obtained elsewhere by Bollicks Robinson, who lent it to James to read. Bollicks always referred to the title of his book as *Balls in the Biggletic*, which added greatly to its virtue.

—

The yardstick used to measure an individual boy or girl's eligibility for receipt of a Sunday school prize was their register of personal attendance at Sunday school. The saintliness or holiness of any inner spirit they might have possessed counted for not a lot. It was presumably felt, both by the Sunday school teachers and by the vicar, that if a boy or a girl attended Sunday school often enough, then at least some of what the Sunday school had to offer would rub off on him or her.

Regularity of attendance at Sunday school was recorded on a list in a register, maintained, when it was not in use, in the church vestry. On any given Sunday in the year (there were no holidays from Sunday school), the Sunday school teacher placed a glorious tick in the register against the names of those present. A condemnatory cross was set against the names of those who were absent. This was a clear example of a cross in the church not always having a benign association.

To confirm the ticks, all in attendance at Sunday school were issued with an adhesive perforated stamp, removed individually from a large sheet of the same. The stamps were a lot bigger than those sold by Miss Jinny Hills and Mrs Olive Bate down in the Fore Street post office for sticking on letters, and they were much more brightly coloured than Jinny and Olive's stamps as well. On its gaudy face the Sunday school stamp contained a Bible scene and text appropriate to the title of the relevant Sunday in accordance with the dictates of the Church calendar.

At the start of the year on the first Sunday in January, all Sunday school pupils were issued with a personal attendance book marked out with rectangles on which future stamps were required to be stuck in sequence as they were received, Sunday after Sunday. Insertion of a stamp in an attendance book was carried out with much cautious licking and grimacing at the rather fishy flavour of the stamp glue.

The stamps provided an immensely powerful guarantee of steady attendances at Sunday school. Every stamp stuck in an attendance book marked an important step towards the next Christmas party and additionally offered proof to parents that boys and girls kicked out of the house on Sunday afternoons to go to Sunday school had dutifully served their time. No one wished to have an attendance book with gaps in it.

Owners zealously guarded their attendance books as they built up, page by page, into a bright record of time spent in the pursuit of religious knowledge, even if the minds of those spending that time were focussed largely on how soon that time would pass so that the attendance book owners could head off and be elsewhere.

―――

A long-term Sunday school teacher at St Peter's, from whose fair hands the stamps were issued with such reluctance that they might have been pure gold dust, was Miss Tyler, a good lady who had left the first flush of youth a long way behind in her streaming wake. Miss Tyler lived with her two sisters, both of a similarly accelerating age, in a house out towards the end of the Terrace, overlooking Port Gaverne.

Miss Tyler's approach to Sunday school teaching had, not unsurprisingly when it was considered what she had to contend with from her pupils, a great deal of shortness of temper about it. However, even through a certain amount of foam might cheer her lips as she ranted in vain at the inattention of her pupils, Miss Tyler, unlike her counterparts at the real school down in Fore Street, could not bring to bear on the pupils any credible threat of physical violence, even if she had wanted to.

For a start, Sunday school took place inside St Peter's church. The church was allegedly a place of sanctuary and peace. Moreover, although the pupils were not in attendance at Sunday school entirely by their own choice, none of them were required in law to be in attendance, unless the law of parents counted. The pupils therefore held in their own hands the final sanction of being able to bugger off if the going got too heavy, assuming they had already got hold of the current Sunday stamp.

―――

Under Miss Tyler's enthusiastic tuition, there were some Sunday school pupils who frequently brought up the issue of the plight of the underprivileged of the world, notwithstanding that a certain number of those very pupils could be numbered among the latter. Jesus loved them all, said Miss Tyler, just like he loved the children of Port Isaac.

From the reference to the poor it only took a quick breath to slip into the subject of peasants. Miss Tyler could then engage in her chapter and verse performance on peasants and peasantry. She pronounced "peasant" as "pheasant", and was thereby induced to provide the balm of giggles to relieve the itch of the Sunday school session. The more times Miss Tyler could be brought to talk about pheasants toiling in fields, the better it was.

———

Miss Tyler was unique among Sunday school teachers in being able to raise a few notes on the church harmonium to accompany Sunday school hymn singing. Her music and the words the pupils sang to it were reluctant companions, however, rarely starting in a synchronised manner and never managing to finish in a dead heat.

Hartland Road, Port Isaac

25

Over the Watershed

JAMES'S FIRST SIGHT of a television set occurred in the celebrated St Andrew's Hotel at the far end of the Terrace. St Andrew's was located almost at the remotest limit of Port Isaac, with Port Gaverne in clear view there at the bottom of the hill below.

The proprietors of St Andrew's were Mr and Mrs Alf Taylor. Alf was an accomplished carpenter whose informed appreciation of the working characteristics of wood was not well matched by his extent of knowledge about very much other than wood. The intellect backing such clear success as St Andrew's enjoyed was primarily the property of Mrs Alf Taylor.

The occasion on which a television set was unveiled at St Andrew's, a golden calf delivered to the awe-struck, was a well-attended afternoon birthday party for Mr and Mrs Alf Taylor's elder son, Dudley.

Dudley, a year older than James, was nicknamed "Monk". This was a nickname of uncertain derivation, although Dudley was such a lugubrious looking boy that that may have had something to do with it. Monk's features were pendulous. A look at Monk and a look at Alf and at Alf's brother Cecil, who dabbled in second-hand furniture for sale to the unwary, eliminated any shred of doubt that the three were related.

Monk was equipped with the type of nose that could be guaranteed to warm the heart of Jimmy Durante, or perhaps

245

even to rival the appendage that the popular cartoon character Chad stuck over a fence in a gesture to lift the national spirit in times of shortage. Chad gave voice to such memorable declarations as "Wot, no bananas?"

Chad was known to additionally query "Wot, no soap?" from his vantage point behind the fence, although there were not many in Port Isaac who were inclined to worry about the scarcity of that particular commodity.

———

Monk's birthday party was lively and enjoyable. Mr and Mrs Alf Taylor were very well off in comparison to the parents of most of the Port Isaac boys and girls invited to the party. The rooms at St Andrew's were an awful lot bigger than those which the boys and girls were used to at home, the party decorations were more lavish and profuse than those they were accustomed to, and not only were the birthday refreshments unusually plentiful but they also demonstrated some exciting variety.

Shortly before five o'clock in the afternoon, the birthday party festivities were halted and the whole complement of the invited guests was shepherded by Mr and Mrs Alf Taylor into what was probably a drawing room if the bulky and uncomfortable looking furniture and the impression that the room gave of being seldom used was anything to go on.

———

The guests were marshalled together in an arc-like cluster, standing or sitting as best they could on the floor (a carpeted floor no less) before what seemed to be a tall wooden box with a small bulging rectangle of greenish glass set into the upper half of its front. Beneath the swell of glass a few blackish brown knobs were grouped in a line.

The glass rectangle was not much bigger than one of the handkerchiefs that a few of the boys among those assembled could probably have pulled from one of their trouser pockets if requested. For other boys the sleeve of a jacket or cuff of a shirt made a preferred substitute for a handkerchief. If produced, any handkerchief would in all likelihood be seen to match the glass rectangle in colour as well as in size.

Alf twisted one of the knobs on the front of the box, and after a heavily nervous interval in which nothing much seemed to be happening came the eerie moment when the glass began to assume a luminous greenish white glow.

For the next half hour the boys and girls were transfixed by the view, displayed on the little television screen – for that was what the green glass rectangle turned out to be – of a cowboy film starring Tex Ritter.

The film was the type of "singing cowboy" offering that would surely have been met by the boys with howls of derision had they been seated on the sixpenny benches of the Rivoli cinema. However, there in that imposingly formal drawing room of St Andrew's guest house, any catcalling at the screen was very far from their minds.

This was different. If this was television it was a revelation. This was something that the children had imagined only ever taking place in stories. There they all were, face to face with a miracle.

The hue of their envy for Monk, who had this marvel in his house to look at every day, at least for the precious few hours during which there was regular broadcasting, eclipsed not only the greenness of the screen but also even the richness of the green hue of crusty snot on those pocket handkerchiefs.

———

From that momentous occasion onwards, not one of Monk's guests who was present would come to feel fully at ease until the day dawned when one of those television boxes appeared within their own homes. Tex Ritter, even with a song or two, provided them all with a defining moment in life opening unimagined consequences for the future.

For all that the wonder of television had appeared on the scene in Port Isaac, its speed of flow towards adoption as a universal home information and entertainment medium moved at a much slower pace than that of the Lake driven to the harbour by Mr Ned Cowlyn's expertise with the flush, irrespective of the many impassioned entreaties Monk's birthday guests made back in their own homes.

———

If Mr and Mrs Alf Taylor were the first to purchase a home television set in Port Isaac, then the second to do so, or at any rate a close second, were Mr and Mrs Jack Spry. Jack, who lived in one of the new council houses in Hartland Road, was the son of Harold, the coalman.

The arrival of Jack's television set created an excitement in the hearts of his neighbours that reached much greater heights when an aerial shaped like a giant letter "H" was erected on Jack's council house chimney. It was an excitement, however, that did not immediately translate itself into any action to emulate and keep up with Jack in the way that it might have done with respect to more mundane matters such as digging the garden or painting the front door.

———

James, for whom the encounter with Mr and Mrs Alf Taylor's television set at St Andrew's was akin to love at first sight, now and then, accompanied by one or two companions, crept along Hartland Road under a cloak of autumn darkness in order to check on the availability of a chink of light showing through Jack Spry's front room window curtains.

In the event that Mrs Jack Spry was less assiduous than usual in drawing her front room curtains together against the onset of darkness, James and his companions were able to move in and take turns to peep one-eyed through the unwitting chink at whatever was showing on the flickering screen of Jack's television set standing in the far corner of the room. They couldn't hear anything, but it was deemed satisfying enough for them just to see the movement on the screen.

Their greatest feat, heedless of the prevailing cold, was to watch an entire *Any Questions?* programme through a gap in the curtains. They saw Freddie Grisewood sitting in the chair and were able to put a face to that great broadcaster, who until then they had only known from his voice on the wireless programme of the same name.

———

A few houses up on the opposite side of Hartland Road to where Mr and Mrs Jack Spry watched their television screen, oblivious to the fact that they were part of a larger audience, was the home of Mr and Mrs Arthur Dinner. Mrs Dinner was named Gladys. Their son was Warren, otherwise known as Flynner.

Arthur, although very much a man of the people, was well and truly shaped by Gladys to fit with Gladys's requirements.

Gladys was prim, purse-mouthed and proper, endowed with a steely tongue rivalling Tom Brown's clasp knife for sharpness and the whole St Peter's PT Club under CPO Arthur Welch for its commitment to strenuous exercise. When Gladys was friendly to them, people watched their backs if they were sensible. When Gladys was their enemy, they ran; it didn't matter where to as long as it was away from her.

———

If Arthur had ever tried to flee from Gladys, he must have forgotten when it was since Arthur had long ago decided that escape was impossible. For him the war with Gladys was over. Arthur was resigned to sit out his incarceration for the remaining duration. He became a placid and reclusive man living in a nutshell of his own construction, off which Gladys's invective directed both at him and so many others bounced with impunity.

Gladys was the doyenne of those who chose to lurk behind the curtains in their front room bay windows to spy on the passing parade in the hope of spotting any aberration, no matter how small, which might give her a working edge over the perpetrator. For whatever Gladys saw she found it easy to come up with an assumption that she could elaborate on and distort, and on the rare occasions when she couldn't she was always able to fall back on the fertile field of rumours that graced her mind.

———

Arthur was heavily built, although by no means fat. He had a head of fine brown hair that rolled back in striking waves from a central parting. His life revolved around his exceptionally well tended back garden, the racing pages in his newspaper, boxing commentaries on the wireless, a chain-like sequence of fags, and isolating himself from Gladys as best he could.

For Arthur it seemed that the trivial round and the common task really did furnish all he ought to ask (inasmuch as anything could be asked with Gladys present) to deny himself a road in the near vicinity. However, life took a turn for the better for Arthur in the best possible way when the television set arrived at Jack Spry's council house down the road.

———

Arthur got his own television set installed not much later. With that in hand, Arthur was able to construct his entire day around the few hours of television programming. Outside of those precious moments, he was perfectly prepared to stare in anticipation and investigate the nuances of the test card. *Watch with Mother* was just what the doctor might have ordered to fill in Arthur's afternoon.

Arthur was so enthralled with what he saw on his television screen one afternoon that he called two council workers from their loitering in Hartland Road to come into his house and look at what was showing. Gladys must have been out somewhere at the time and was clearly not expected to return imminently.

The council workmen, neither of whom had seen a television set previously, did not in any case need any encouragement to stop not working outside and continue not working inside Arthur's house.

Arthur and the council workmen all gazed, sitting comfortably in their seats, at an episode of *Muffin the Mule*. Following that, it was necessary for the council workmen to return to their pretence of work for another hour or so. They were asked, by an interested party, what they thought about what they had just seen, and in a very perceptive critical review they declared that not only was it marvellous but children might also have enjoyed the exploits of Muffin.

───

In his pursuit of perfect television reception, something of a contradiction in terms where he was concerned, Arthur tinkered a lot with the position and orientation of the aerial mounted on his chimney, as well as with the picture controls on his television set. His rate of success was just about as limited as was Gladys's innate goodwill to all men.

Arthur therefore became an overly frequent caller on the local electrical engineer who had installed his television set. This was, incidentally, James's father, Bill. Arthur came to Bill bearing plaintive requests for the abolition of snow from his screen, or otherwise to stop his picture either rolling like a wheel or leaning sideways as if it were drunk.

One morning, Arthur appeared in Hartland Road swinging a length of coaxial cable in one hand, while enthusing at how a picture of a man smoking a fag could be grabbed out of the air so as to slide down along that very cable to emerge, spread out like lemon curd (a spread regarded by those like James who didn't appreciate it as "phlegm and turd") across the screen of his television set.

───

Arthur entered his dream element when amateur boxing contests were featured on his television set. He could then lean back in his chair in a degree of comfort and watch the boxing bill progress all the way through the ranks from flyweight to the much-anticipated heavyweight contest.

Arthur was a dedicated follower of the inappropriately named "noble art", and was blessed with an encyclopaedic fund of background information that set him alight when he chose to pass it on.

Professional boxing was still very much the province of the wireless, on which medium it was typified by the notoriously subjective but always articulate commentating style of Raymond Glendenning, against whom the all too soporific inter-round summaries by W. Barrington Dalby (known as "Barry") acted as a counterpoint.

Arthur Dinner was one of the many who sat up well into the small hours of the morning to listen to fight commentaries by Raymond coming in over the crackling and whistling airwaves all the way from America. Raymond was ever ready to describe how yet another brave British heavyweight had been robbed of a title in spite of his having being knocked out in one of the early rounds.

—

When life eventually stopped moving Arthur along its path, he was set free for a while up in St Endellion graveyard. Then Gladys passed along the same route and was buried in on top of Arthur. Sometimes even the grave didn't let its customers escape the vicissitudes of their lives.

—

One day, the King died too. One of the consequences of his untimely demise was an announcement that the Coronation of the King's daughter, destined to become Queen Elizabeth II, would be broadcast in its entirety on the television screen. Moreover, the broadcast would be a so-called "live" event, meaning that those who were confronted by active television sets at the time would see the order of service of the Coronation exactly as it took place.

Some said that a live broadcast of the Coronation would give those who saw it the feeling that they were actually there in the abbey church, along with the royalty, lords, ladies, invited dignitaries and quite imposing members of the clerical hierarchy. It sounded quite breathtaking.

Since most of those who offered this opinion had yet to see a live television broadcast (or for that matter any television broadcast at all), how they knew about the atmospheric characteristics that they talked of could only be guessed at. Perhaps those among them who could read had read about it by accident rather than design as they riffled through a newspaper on the way to the vital racing page. Possibly Arthur Dinner started it all off as yet another rumour.

The monumental importance of the announcement that the Coronation was to be broadcast live on television provided a definitive kick up the ass to all the fence sitters and those hitherto hesitant to acquire their very own television sets. It goaded them firstly into a scramble and afterwards into an unrestrained gallop to get a home installation made in time.

Of course, the King passed away about a year and a half before his daughter's coronation actually took place, so it wasn't really that the interim period during which a television set could be acquired was all that short, it was just that the only time that ever counted in the "dreckly" culture of Port Isaac was the last few minutes.

As far as James was concerned, the death of the King passed him by. On the very day of the King's expiry, the sixth of February, 1952, James was mandated to attend a clinic in Bodmin with his mother to undertake a periodic preventive screening against tuberculosis. The prospect of journeying all the way to Bodmin was a major undertaking that had focussed both of their minds for some days in advance of departure.

The highlight at the clinic was for James to have his chest X-rayed, in the hope that thereafter, features ominously referred to as "shadows" would not appear on the X-ray photos.

James was well prepared for the visit to the Bodmin clinic. He was wearing clean underwear, as he always did when he went far away from home. His mother prescribed clean underpants in case James should happen to be run over by a car. Any injuries that he might sustain in such an accident would be as nothing compared to the shame that would fall on James and his family if on subsequent examination by a doctor he was found to be wearing skid-marked underpants.

———

On the return of James and his mother from Bodmin, Maureen Collings, James's mother's cousin, came along from a day of dodging the manager at the Co-op where she worked and said to his mother, "Isn't it sad about the King?" Thus it was that James came to hear the bad news.

It was strange that, all through the day up to the point of Maureen's appearance, taking into account the journey to and from Bodmin, the wait in the clinic for his turn to be examined, and a look at and in some of the shops set along the drear prospect of Bodmin's main street, not one word of the loss of the King had managed to filter through to James. His own and his mother's preoccupations for the day must have been quite intense.

———

Immediately following the death of the King, the whole world seemed drenched in mournful gloom. Feet dragged, as if they were pushing through black treacle. Cold February reigned supreme. No one ever wrote a song about February. The King was gone, rationing was a daily reality, and the shadows of the war were still fingering in, looking as long as the shadows of stark elms on snow at a winter sunset.

On the other hand, just as when altar candles were supposed to be snuffed out there was usually a residual spark of hope to spring eternal on the candlewicks, life went on in spite of setbacks. A poet with the altogether wonderful name of Percy Bysshe

Shelley wrote, in a poem that James learned at school, that when winter comes, spring can't be too far behind. And it was so.

Many of the Port Isaac boys wondered how Percy Bysshe Shelley had got on at the school that he attended. His fate, had he turned up in the playground of Port Isaac County Primary school with a name like that, would have been too awful to contemplate.

———

The King was dead, long live the Queen, and now what was needed was to see her coronation broadcast on television. The first half of the year 1953 was therefore as much a period of great excitement for purveyors of television sets as it was for their customers.

The purchase of a television set was very much eased with recourse to the modern option of hire purchase, known for short as "HP". HP was a scheme also not inappropriately referred to as the "never-never". Those who took it up came to discover that they never seemed to quite manage to reach a stage where their debt was paid off and the television set finally became theirs.

James's mother had a deeply instilled horror of incurring any financial indebtedness to anyone for any reason. In her view, to owe someone something made her beholden to him and placed a stigmatic load on her shoulders that could surely not be borne. She inherited this quality, determining that what she didn't have and couldn't afford to buy she could do without and wouldn't miss, from Gran and Granfer Creighton.

James's father had no such compunction driving him. He was as incompetent a manager of what little money he did have as could be possibly imagined. He was ever willing to acquire things he didn't need with money he didn't have and to leave the consequences to another, namely James's mother, to sort out.

This did not in principle make for a great deal of domestic harmony, not least when the HP television set ordered by his father first arrived at James's home. However, the magical touch of the impending Coronation papered over the cracks after a short period of customary agitation. James and his mother attached themselves to the new television set as tightly as limpets on the rocks around Port Isaac harbour. Fabian of Scotland Yard and the Lone Ranger leapt joyfully at them into their living room.

—

As the great event of the Coronation broadcast live on television drew nearer and nearer, the debate dealing with what was to be anticipated, not only on the television screen but also in terms of the behaviour of those watching at home, reached unprecedented levels of intensity.

The more spiritual aspects of the Coronation ceremony, in particular the partaking of the sacrament of Holy Communion by the Queen, were subjected to a very special scrutiny. It was reported that the sacrament of Holy Communion would be celebrated behind a screen. This, said those who reckoned they knew, was intended to eliminate any sacrilegious intrusion by television viewers who might not at the time be observing the proper decorum.

The vicar made a rare visit to the Sunday school to advise the children that when watching the Coronation on television they must be wearing their best Sunday clothes and be sitting facing the screen with their hands clasped together in reverence.

—

James's father's pronouncement on the matter was not atypical of the universal piety temporarily gripping the population. What had to be avoided at all costs, he said, was anyone watching the Coronation while smoking a fag. What would be even worse he declared, was that anyone might be eating half a pasty whilst the sacrament of Holy Communion was in progress. These pronouncements carried all the more weight coming as they did from a man whom James had yet to see set his foot inside a church door.

Maybe, James thought, if half a pasty was out, then it would be all right to eat a whole pasty during the Coronation Holy Communion, but then he realised that once he had eaten half of a whole he would then be left holding the forbidden half. It was a dilemma, never to be resolved, as he didn't have the opportunity to test the theory out.

———

Standing at attention for "God Save the Queen" did not require any emphasising either from his father or from the vicar, or from anyone else as far as that went, as James was conditioned to do that automatically. Everyone was supposed to stand their ground for the national anthem, and for the most part did when it was unavoidable. There was however a fast growing and rather admired number of those who had learned how to gain the safety of the exit at the conclusion of public events a secure second or two before the national anthem was struck up.

———

The Coronation came and the Coronation went. James sat through every second of the live television broadcast. The picture on the television screen might have been slightly blurry, as if it was just off focus, but James missed nothing of what took place. No fags were observed to be smoked and no half pasties to be eaten all through it. Even Arthur Dinner's television picture behaved itself and shed itself of any real semblance of snow.

When the Coronation ceremony was over, James, in common with so many others, changed from best Sunday clothes back into everyday wear.

———

No one living in Port Isaac ever suspected that along with the Coronation the Sirens were singing. Port Isaac was poised on a pointy watershed between streaming ways of life. The next step was about to transgress a border into unknown territory, and there would be no way back.

Break, break, break,
At the foot of thy crags, O Sea!
But the tender grace of a day that is dead
Will never come back to me.

ALFRED, LORD TENNYSON

Lightning Source UK Ltd.
Milton Keynes UK
UKHW040612280519
343447UK00001B/384/P